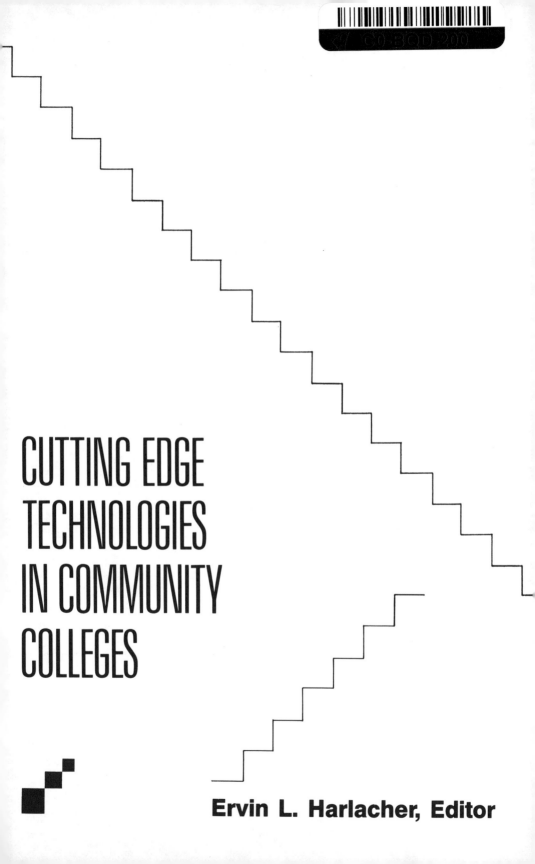

CUTTING EDGE TECHNOLOGIES IN COMMUNITY COLLEGES

Ervin L. Harlacher, Editor

ABOUT THE EDITOR

Ervin L. Harlacher is professor of higher education at Pepperdine University's Graduate School of Education and Psychology. Before coming to Pepperdine in 1983, he held several administrative positions in community colleges across the country. He was the founding president at Brookdale Community College (NJ), Chancellor of the Metropolitan Community Colleges (MO), and President of Marin College (CA). Harlacher is Executive Secretary of COMBASE and a member of several other professional organizations, including the American Educational Research Association and AACJC's Council on Universities and Colleges.

American Association of Community and Junior Colleges
National Center for Higher Education
Suite 410, One Dupont Circle, NW
Washington, D.C. 20036
(202) 293-7050

CONTENTS

■

I.   The Challenge of the Future

II. The State of the Art

III. Future Leadership Requirements

FOREWORD

In its report, *Building Communities,* the Commission on the Future of Community Colleges notes that "the challenge of technology in support of teaching will grow even more intense" in the 21st Century and recommends "that every community college develop a campuswide plan for the use of technology, one in which educational and administrative applications can be integrated."

This monograph, *Cutting Edge Technologies in Community Colleges,* will make a significant contribution to the achievement of that goal. Its content represents a carefully crafted balance between case studies of current uses of technology and exciting glimpses of the future. The authors represent a mix of forward-thinking practitioners whose institutions are making the very best use of current technology and futurists, educators, and industrialists whose ideas, plans, and projections will help lead the way for American higher education into the 21st century.

AACJC is deeply indebted to Control Data Corporation for its generous support of this monograph, to Bernard Luskin, president of American Interactive Media, Inc., for its concept; to Ervin Harlacher, professor of higher education at the Pepperdine University Graduate School of Education and Psychology, and to Andrea Spirtos, Pepperdine doctoral student, for organizing and developing the monograph; and to the authors for their valuable contributions to the continued improvement of America's community, technical, and junior colleges.

Finally, appreciation must be extended to COMBASE, a cooperative for the advancement of community-based postsecondary education, for inviting several of the monograph authors to present their papers at its fall 1987 conference on "Cutting Edge Technologies."

James F. Gollattscheck
Executive Vice President
American Association of Community and
   Junior Colleges
Washington, D.C.

PREFACE

Educators are confronted with the emergence of a new era: the information age. Moving from a post-industrial, "traditional" mode to a technological modality is both time-consuming and costly. In addition, there are many factors to be considered, including changes in the job market, malleable ethics, and a growing need for an educational environment responsive to the lifespan learner.

Another problem is the role of the community college at the close of the 20th century. Twenty-six years ago, there were approximately 678 community colleges serving 500,000 students. Today, there are at least 1,200 community colleges serving 5,000,000 students (Leslie 1986). The increase in the number of students, at least in part, is due to the adult lifelong learner returning to the community college environment.

The National Center for Education Statistics studies indicate that by the year 2000, the population of the United States will be dominated by persons in their middle years: between the ages of thirty and forty-four, with the rising curve of persons between forty-five and sixty-four years of age (Cross, 1981, p. 4). The average American now has three careers during his worklife (McCabe, 1981, p. 22).

The fact that adult education spans more than fifty years (Cross, 1981, p. 9) will have a tremendous impact on community, technical, and junior colleges. The number of adults thirty-five years and older who are enrolled in college programs increased by 66 percent between 1972 and 1978 (Cross, 1981, p. 37).

As the population of the community college changes, so do the goals of the student. Adults returning to education need immediate knowledge to solve day-to-day problems of living (Griffin, 1983, p. 41). The adult learners are responding to a function of their profession and its prescriptions. They must form strategies to maximize their flexibility (Griffin, 1983, p. 76). Education for the adult learner is less a factor of curriculum than it is a relationship between needs-meeting and professionalism.

Diversity, accessibility, transferability, and accountability are essential ingredients of a truly comprehensive system of education, but never more so than when considering the adult learner. It is projected that by 1990, most adults will work a thirty-two-hour week (Cetron, 1986, p. 14). When not at work, many will be in preparation for their next job, upgrading their current skills, or retraining for a new job market. Many community colleges may be open twenty-four hours a day, acting as training centers from 4:00 p.m. to midnight (Cetron, 1986, p. 14). In short, the academic community must be more accessible to the needs of the new-age student in order to cope with the mixture of needs, abilities, backgrounds, schedules, and commitment levels.

The new age, unlike the industrial era, which was characterized by humankind's drive to control things, is driven by a dramatic increase in the availability and complexity of information. The new-age information society does not replace that which went before; it transforms. Information is fungible (freely interchangeable), expandable, substitutable, transportable, diffusible, and most important, not resource-hungry (Cleveland, 1985, p. 16).

If our nation is to remain competitive in the world marketplace, a greater emphasis on high-tech education is needed. This requires not only the dissemination of information, but also the training and retraining of individuals in an ever-changing arena of techno-literacy (Cetron, 1986). In order to realistically fulfill this goal and to consolidate the retraining process with the ongoing needs of business, the community college may be forced to operate on an around-the-clock schedule.

While the initial capital investment may appear to be prohibitive for educational institutions, the benefits far outweigh the costs, as exhibited in the following chapters. The use of television, computers, video discs, interactive video tapes, satellite dishes, teleconferencing, and other high technology methodologies will be discussed. Cutting edge technology requires cutting edge educational technique. The community college must become the razor.

People who do not educate and continue to re-educate themselves to participate in the new knowledge environment will be the peasants of the information society (Cleveland, 1985, p. 21).

Andrea Spirtos
Assistant Editor and Doctoral Student
Pepperdine University
Culver City, California

References

Cetron, Marvin J., Soriano, Barbara, and Gayle, Margaret, "Forecasting American Education" *Educational Digest* 51 (March 1986): 14–17.

Cleveland, Harlan, "Educating the Information Society" *Change* 17 (July/August 1985): 12–21.

Cross, K. Patricia, *Adults as Learners: Increasing Participation and Facilitating Learning* (San Francisco: Jossey-Bass Publishers), 1981.

Griffin, Colin, *Curriculum Theory in Adult and Lifelong Learning* (London: Croom Helm), 1983.

Leslie, Judith, W. et al., *Computers Serving Students: The Community College Way,* CAUSE Monograph Series, CAUSE Publications, 1986.

McCabe, Robert H., et al., "Technology & Education: Policy, Implementation, and Evaluation" *National Conference on Technology and Education* (January 26–28, 1981), p. 22.

PART I:
THE CHALLENGE
OF THE FUTURE

1

EDUCATION AND CURRICULUM FUTURES: IMPACTS FROM TECHNOLOGICAL ADVANCES AND GLOBAL TRENDS

.

By Earl C. Joseph

This chapter is about the future—the future of cutting edge technologies. It will highlight some developing technological trends, emerging issues, and possible breakthroughs and forecasts that affect the short- and long-range futures of community colleges.

The cutting edge of current and forecasted future advances in technology continues to offer community colleges new opportunities in the high-tech information age. Changing world conditions in the new global economy will continue to have an impact on the United States, compelling education to change in ways that meet the challenges posed by this new era. These developments are accelerating and will force major curriculum changes, altering the way education is delivered in the future.

The emergence of artificially intelligent expert systems technology portends radical changes in what is meant by education and in its delivery and schools, including community colleges. That is, expert systems will alter education more than any technology has in the past.

The Information Age Futures

While the final shape of the emerging global future has not solidified, much can be forecasted about its probable character. Certainly a part of the future will be much like it is today. Much of the future will have evolved from our current state, but will be largely unrecognizable in today's terms. Additionally, another part of the future will result from revolutionary developments and breakthroughs unknown today. Of course the farther we forecast into the future the more the latter cases will be the norm.

The United States entered the information age in the late 1950s when, percentage-wise, there were more people working at information-related jobs than at factory jobs. However, the educational system has not yet caught up—the primary curriculum is still pegged to the needs of an industrial era. Today the primary task of most workers (over 70 percent) is to collect, store, process, receive, and disseminate information. But no educational institution—whether elementary, high school, or college—requires that students take a mandatory course in thinking, the primary skill needed

3

in handling information. Our society is an information driven society—politically, socially, culturally, and economically. Therefore, citizens should consider it a criminal offense that our schools are not preparing students in the key skill area needed for the "new" information era. Forecasts indicate that before the 1990s are concluded, well over 90 percent of the United States population will be working at information-intense jobs.

The cutting edge of computerized information technologies—including office automation, expert systems, computer assisted design, computer assisted manufacturing, computer assisted engineering, computerized numerical control, word processing and text editing, spread sheets, and many others—are but the tip of the iceberg of the new information age. These technologies are transforming jobs, businesses, financial institutions, factories, offices, government, and science. They are just beginning their impact on education. They have entered the classroom. They will soon alter the way education will be delivered. They are powerful tools for amplifying the student's learning, the teacher's teaching, and the services of school administrators and staff.

Since information and knowledge are the "economic engines of growth," it is useful to investigate the rate of information and knowledge growth. Back at the turn of the century, in the year 1900, the production rate for new knowledge creation was doubling the amount of new knowledge worldwide every fifty years. This estimate was derived from counting the number of patents issued by governments and by analyzing the number of scientific and technical papers published. Knowledge now doubles every five years, according to Alvin Toffler (1980) in his book *The Third Wave,* and we almost double the amount of information in use yearly.

This is a lot of new knowledge creation. It means that in the next five years society could match the total amount of knowledge that it has produced from its beginning! Some basic things happen when this knowledge is applied. First, it causes change. Since we are accelerating the rate of knowledge production, we are also accelerating change. Second, the application of new knowledge allows us to do what we have been doing more efficiently, with less input of capital, energy, materials and labor. Thus, there is no doubt that when we apply new knowledge, one major result is to displace people from jobs. Third, new knowledge provides society with the means to do some things that were impossible to do in the past because we didn't know how; when new knowledge is applied for this purpose new jobs are created. At the rate society is producing new knowledge, there should be no lack of jobs for the future—if that knowledge is applied to do new things.

The information age is transforming society into a "high-wage economy" requiring education, and especially community colleges, to raise their sights from preparing students for a low-wage economy toward preparing students to enter this new high-wage economic age.

4

High-Tech Age Futures

There are about fifteen high-tech areas of the economy. Among them are computers, office equipment, telecommunications, medical technology, tools and instruments, robots, bio-genetics, space and aerospace, electronic components, exotic materials, and factory automation equipment. This area of the economy has historically grown rapidly, almost twice as fast as the rest of the economy, but on an up-and-down trajectory. Today the high-tech portion of the economy amounts to about 20 percent, but since it is growing faster, it should represent about 30 to 35 percent in ten years.

As such, it has become society's most important area for new job creation. Thus, community colleges must learn to do a better job in preparing students for this job market—and to use cutting edge high-tech in the educational delivery process.

Computer Age Futures

The computer has gone through many advances and changes since the early 1950s. Sizewise, the computer has changed from roomfuls of equipment to desktops; soon portables will be common. The cost has tumbled from about a million dollars per box to thousands, and soon computers costing a few tens of dollars will be more capable than those costing over a million today. Once, interface access was only through a human programmer and operator; now computers have become end-user friendly and soon intelligent systems will be the norm. Software was once limited; now there are lots of alternatives for a growing list of application areas with many expert systems beginning to hit the scene. Hardware was centralized in computer rooms; now it is being distributed with much of it being networked through communication systems providing easy access. Memory was very limited and costly. Now most computers have lots of memory at low cost and greater amounts will be available soon at very inexpensive prices. Computer input (access), once effected via impossible-to-read manual tapes and cards, is now facilitated by user-friendly screens and keyboards. Around the corner are speech discourse systems and source data automated capture systems. In the past only the big institution could afford computers; now they are common in the small businesses and in a growing number of schools. Soon almost everyone will be able to afford them.

With this much change in only three and a half decades, the impact of computers on society has been great. Now they are poised to fantastically affect education within the next decade.

Robot Age Futures

The robots are coming—even in education. Robots in factories work cheaper and produce consistently higher quality work than humans do on some jobs. Robots are becoming smarter and more intelligent and, as

5

they do so, they cost less (work even cheaper). People, on the other hand, expect and deserve higher pay as soon as they become more educated and experienced. Since society is driven by economic considerations, smarter and more intelligent robots must take over more complex jobs from humans in the future. Humans will need to stay ahead of robot capabilities in the future and move into jobs that robots can't handle. This means that community colleges will be needed more in the future—to retrain the vast numbers of people to be displaced by robots.

Already robots are designed and tested for applications outside of factories. Soon the cutting edge of robots will include smart and intelligent ones for use in schools, homes, hospitals, offices, restaurants, grocery and department stores, repair shops, and for many other applications. Imagine robot teacher and administrator aides in the not-too-distant future in community colleges!

Electronic Information Age Futures

Videoconferencing, computer conferencing, electronic or computer bulletin boards, computer mail, information utilities, compact discs, video disc and video cassette libraries, smart telephones, fiber optic communication highways, desktop publishing, portable computers and televisions, knowledge-based systems, and discoursing hardware are the cutting edge of electronic information technology. Each in its own unique way presents new opportunities for community colleges. In a recent study conducted by this writer for the United States Office of Technology Assessment, over 2,000 electronic information technologies were identified! Most are on an explosive growth path which will make obsolete most traditional modes of information handling and information transmission processes—especially for education.

Bio-Engineering Era Futures

For almost thirty years our society has been able to read the "program of life," DNA, and for nearly the last fifteen years it has been able to intervene by cutting and splicing it. This gives us the ability to alter, redesign, and repair all forms of life and to create new life or species. Soon we will have the capacity to produce even more superior human life. Shouldn't every student leave school with knowledge in this increasingly important area? Why? Because they and their loved ones will be radically impacted by this new science. This means that the future community college must provide access for all students to the cutting edge bio-engineering technologies so that they will know what they are capable of.

Global Economy Age Futures

We have become an interconnected world relative to the economy, and this means that all students need to be literate about international economics. Here again the cutting edge technologies of computer networks, coupled with global economy simulation software, would facilitate students' learning about this important area. Since the United States is so unprepared educationally for this era, Japan and other countries are having a seriously negative impact, a trend we don't want to continue. To reverse this trend will require a much bigger role from education.

Today our country has more goods flowing over the Pacific Ocean than the Atlantic—therefore, we have entered the Pacific age. This means that from here on out and for a long time to come the United States will be increasingly affected by trade with the Pacific Rim nations. Community colleges need to teach more foreign languages and cultures—especially as they relate to the Pacific Rim nations—if the United States is expected to cope in such a future. Many more U.S. citizens need to read the journals, written in their respective languages, from these countries. The cutting edge electronic information technologies of personal computers, networks, software, data bases, automated language translation, foreign language and cultural history training compact discs, automated readers and scanners, (and the like) can greatly help students and teachers in this task of keeping abreast and ahead of developments coming from these other nations.

Medical Revolution Era Futures

Since the turn of this century medical advances have nearly doubled the average life expectancy. This means we have more careers throughout our lives. The baby boomers are swelling the ranks of the middle-aged and will someday place a population bulge in the ranks of the elderly. These adults will increasingly need community colleges, which will have to deliver education along much greater economies of scale. The use of cutting edge technologies must be sped up to increase the productivity of education. That is, the older society becomes, the longer our lives, the more education is needed.

Education for the Futures

From the foregoing it should now be obvious that each of us needs to be schooled with the abilities, skills, techniques, methods, processes, philosophies, and knowledge needed to understand emerging trends and issues. This is especially important as change comes ever faster; each individual needs to be skilled in futures studies (anticipatory sciences). Such skills enable individuals to better use computers and to answer the "what if" type questions that the future poses for our society.

Technology Trends and Some Future Forecasted Impacts

The basic cutting edge technology "engine of change" is the "more-for-less" techno-economic equation. As each technology advances, this equation allows or forces a trend curve into the future, creating more intelligent and capable systems for less cost. This "more-for-less" equation also spawns more competition—clones, plug compatibles, and new generations of competing systems—which forces the industry to respond with advanced changes to their systems in order to meet their competitors' thrusts. As a result, wave after wave of improved products and services come faster and faster.

The cutting edge of technology will thus continue to change, resulting in (1) drastic cost reductions, but on a roller-coaster pricing path; (2) dramatic performance improvement and an explosive functionality growth; (3) higher efficiency and quality; (4) rapid public acceptability and attendant deep educational, social, and economic impacts; (5) fantastic developments in user-friendly systems; and (6) a rapid growth in new business opportunities.

Emerging Issues

For community colleges these technological forces of change provide both opportunities and problems. How will the colleges keep up-to-date hardware in their classrooms, labs, and offices if technologies change and advance rapidly? How can teachers be kept up-to-date?—only through the use of newer and newer user-friendly technology. Where will colleges find the funds?—perhaps in a major way only by using these modern technologies to raise their productivity. For example, the typical Japanese classroom has twice as many students per educator, but Japanese students do significantly better than those in the United States on IQ tests. This tells us that cutting edge technology for community colleges can be advantageously used for amplifying learning and reducing costs so that funds can be released to improve education.

Of course there are many other emerging issues and forces-of-change that community colleges will face in the future. What part of education should be performed in the classroom, and what proportion should be delivered via "real-time" educational technology outside of the classroom? What is the basic curriculum for the information age—what must a student learn to be considered educated in the information age? What is the future role of community colleges? Is it different for different regions?

Possible Breakthroughs

There are many "what if" possible breakthroughs, "trump cards," that may become technically and economically feasible, thus taking over as the norm.

For example, one such trump card assumes a future of very user-friendly portable personal computers with several compact discs. These systems are also capable of speech discourse (speech recognition and speech output backed up with "intelligence") and have access to a wide variety of knowledge bases (access to almost the totality of society's amassed knowledge). Let's call this a "current awareness system." Assume further that it takes the initiative (without waiting for the user to call it into action) by sensing the user's needs (and if it doesn't understand the sensory information it gets, it asks questions). Additionally, when it understands how it can be of assistance to its user, it dips into its knowledge base, or the network's knowledge utility service, to obtain the knowledge needed by its user. Then it makes the user aware of the knowledge by offering advice. Of course, the design of such a system is critical, or else it will end up being a nag and lapse into disuse.

Such a system is now feasible for future development. When it is in common use, what then will be the role of the community colleges? There is little doubt that there will be a role; however, one thing is sure: it will be very different than today.

Assuming the existence of either expert systems or highly integrated current awareness systems in the future, the more basic question becomes "what is the role of humans in such a future?" If we further assume that these systems are designed and used as tools to amplify humans, then the answer to both of these questions is straightforward—there is a definite and growing role.

Why? When such systems are used as an advice-giving consultive tool, then the human has access to all the knowledge that the tool has plus the additional information in one's head. The combination creates a synergy, affording the human access to more knowledge than the machine. This means humans will always be needed over and above a machine society and that they will always be more capable! For some jobs, however, the machine will be sufficient. Therefore, in such a future, there is only one answer for humans: to stay ahead of machines. It is education, but not just any old education, that will allow this to happen. An educational system is needed that is specifically designed for such an age.

Implied Community College Alternative Futures

The cutting edge of personal computers and networks has put society into a world of distributed systems. They are forcing business, government, and society at large to decentralize. In addition, adults are often being displaced from their jobs. This adds up to the growing need for more community colleges—if they focus on recareering, and not simply initial job training.

As computer networks grow in massive use, with very low cost personal computers, television graphics, compact disc memory and lots of educational software, an alternative will exist for students—especially older students. They will be able to use their portable networked personal computers as "real-time educators" instead of going to a physical or rooted school building. Will this happen? You can bet on it—in fact it's starting!

9

Longer-Range Futures for Community Colleges

There is a great need for each of us to have a great deal more education than we have. Someday, perhaps sooner than later, our society will recognize that a high school education is not nearly enough education. Perhaps it will become mandatory for everyone to re-enter formalized education throughout one's life. When this happens, community colleges will need to rapidly expand their system, role, curriculum, and sites.

However, on the other side of the cutting edge technological advances are the strides now being made with expert systems. There is little doubt about their ability to raise the productivity of human experts and professionals. This means that professionals will be deskilled when society massively applies expert systems. That is, if there is x amount of work to be done which today would take y professionals to do it, future expert systems will make it possible to undertake the same amount of work with considerably fewer than y professionals. Fortunately, as new knowledge increases, new jobs are created that require many more professionals.

This deskilling of the professional creates a number of problems. The first is the problem of job displacement, which requires professionals who are displaced to retrain. This trend puts the pressure on community colleges to provide a curriculum to meet this challenge. The second problem is the one of new jobs. Society is speeding up its production of new knowledge fast enough so that enough new jobs could be made to keep well ahead of the displacement problem, *if* our institutions (public or private, business, education, government, etc.) change fast enough to allow the new jobs a place in their ranks. If they do not, then most of our new knowledge will go into doing things more efficiently, causing most job displacement. In order to compete economically, we will be forced to create new jobs in expert systems, genetic engineering, and many other technologies which, in turn, will require transitions in community colleges to meet the challenges posed. If this doesn't happen, the United States will slide down the ranks of the developed nations and become, even before the year 2000, a third world, third-rate nation.

Conclusion

Forecasting is a discipline which considers fundamental questions about possible futures in such a way that no matter what alternative futures are forecasted, one can give compellng reasons or grounds for the likely occurrence of what *could* happen, not *predictions* for what *will* happen. The fundamental philosophical questions of what educational futures are possible are linked to such questions as: What futures should we design and implement? What technologies should we use to deliver education in the future? But before we can answer these questions, we must first answer the question: What is the role of education in and for the future? Once we answer this question, then we have a method for determining which technologies we should design and use in the future community college. In this chapter, these questions were largely ignored. Instead some future directions, together with some of their expected impacts, were covered as needed background information.

The idea that there is a single firm, unchanging, and absolute future is alien to futurists. In reality, there are many possible alternative futures. Our problem is to choose and design the "best" ones. Accordingly, the basis for discovering possible futures lies not in isolated forecasts, but in a research and development program for designing alternative futures. There is only one answer for a brighter tomorrow: education. But in order to add all of the things suggested in the foregoing, to find the means (people and dollars) to do so, we must use technology to raise the productivity of educational institutions, elsewise we will never be able to afford the education we need.

Reference

Toffler, Alvin, *The Third Wave* (New York, NY: William Morrow), 1980.

Earl C. Joseph is a futurist and president of Anticipatory Sciences, Inc., St. Paul, Minnesota.

2

THE SOCIOLOGICAL IMPLICATIONS OF THE NEW TECHNOLOGY

.

By Bernard G. Kirsch

There is a myth in our society that if it is new, it must be good. Accordingly, negative impact of the use of new technology on environment, privacy, morality, cultures, and traditions has not, until recently, been considered with the result that much damage has been done to the human condition. The emphasis on quantity of life rather than on quality of life has been a major thrust of technology and so-called modern "advancement."

Many issues will not go away and have become increasingly important as more and more sophisticated technology comes on the scene. The areas of energy, communication and computer use, genetic experimentation, and pollution have been proliferating at a geometric rate. The concept of progress, however, is now being challenged with talk of limited growth and questions about whether material progress is really the way of salvation. The challenge comes from many scientists and economists, among others.

Advancing technology has intensified an ancient problem: the unintended consequences of our actions. As technology becomes more powerful, its unintended consequences become more numerous and more important. The hidden effects of technology and the application of technology weigh heavily on the value of new "advancements."

Most articles on the future of technology do not discuss policy affecting life-style and human implications. This is gradually changing as the effects of new technologies become more and more apparent.

If we look at the changes in human relations carried by technological advances, we can see similar changes taking place. They may not always be reflected in policy decisions, but many decisions regarding education and social services, for example, are a result of technological changes.

Willis Harman (1979) has said that "we find that we came through this period of centuries during which our technology and modernization trend brought us many things, but we also have a counterpart which has a negative cast." He continued, "Special implications of this modernization have brought us new forms of scarcity such as fresh air, fresh water and physical resources."

These scarcities have also caused threats to health, a disruption of natural balances, and the dominance of large institutions over individuals. The increasingly autonomous character of economic and technological

13

institutions threatens democracy as they take on global status without the concomitant responsibilities to the citizens of the world.

As these technological changes affect our daily lives, rarely do we take the time to analyze their impact on the human and community structure or the serious dilemmas for individuals needing to make ethical choices where technological development and human values collide.

Let us now examine one issue and look at its implications as it develops. The "information-oriented" society, as far as one can imagine it today, will be more sophisticated and technologically advanced, more integrated, and more complex than any of the societies we know today in Japan, North America, and Western Europe. The information society is also beginning to spread throughout Southeast Asia, Africa, and Latin America.

In an information society, inter-relationships and interdependencies among various classes, groups, and segments of society will be more numerous; so much so, that it will be increasingly difficult for society to maintain a democratic character and internal equilibrium.

Tomorrow, it will be within the reach of a determined minority to dominate the system by seizing control of information mechanisms. Remember the old piece of wisdom that information is power. The issue of information "haves" and "have-nots" has become explosive, not only at national levels, but also at global levels.

Communications technology's influence on society is not new. The telegraph, the telephone, the radio, and the Gutenberg Press all triggered major changes to society and cultures. The new technologies and developments have led to similar confrontations, but on an even greater and more complex scale. For example, the issue of computer development and its implications are vast and critical. There have been advances in the protection of privacy through specific legislative acts, but still greater assurances are needed. There are many political and historical examples of abuse of personal data. Public policy should be shaped by these present and past experiences.

The communications technology and its promise of a million-fold increases in man's capacity to handle information undoubtedly will have the most far-reaching consequences of any contemporary development. The potential for good in this technology and the danger inherent in its misuse exceed our ability to imagine. Computers can be looked at as Machiavellian mechanical overlords that may ultimately enslave or destroy the human race. The specter of computerized invasion of privacy arose with the proposed centralization of federal statistical services in the United States in the mid-sixties. In the wake of computerized billing, banking, and recordkeeping at local and national levels, not enough hue and cry has been raised over the depersonalization and dehumanization of the numbered person.

The public's stake in the destiny of computers is overwhelming. Computers have some obvious roles to play in education, mass communications,

14

politics, ecology, and economy; they play less obvious but vital roles in the enhancement of human intelligence, in global population control, the evolution of democracy, and the amelioration of human misery.

Plans for making the benefits of computers available to all are long overdue. Democratic dialogue on the public issues at stake in charting the long-range evolution of computers for the benefit of all of us is of prime importance. An evaluation of the potential of computer science and technology in meeting the challenge of spiraling social problems is sorely needed. The domain of man-computer problem solving is unarticulated and unexplored, even though everyone piously professes that computers will extend human intellect.

The misanthropic stance of computer "experts" needs to be replaced by computer professionals who are responsive to the social responsibilities of their calling. This may mean housekeeping and the setting up of ethical and professional standards for managers, system analysts, programmers, computer operators, and other computer specialists. It may mean humanizing the departments of computer and information science in our universities, making them more responsive to interdisciplinary social problems.

The triple threat of an uninformed public, a technologically rather than humanistically oriented computer world, and spiraling social problems pose the fundamental challenge facing a practical public philosophy for the transition toward a computer-serviced society. Mass information utilities are expanding with the extension of interactive computer systems to the general public at home, school, and office. We can't ignore the concomitant effect of human isolation, manipulation, homogeneity of the population, and subliminal control.

An example of social experimentation with communication technology is found in the planning of the prototype Qube, an experiment in Columbus, Ohio, that has been given wide publicity. The information services include public areas of education, voting, and municipal activities as well as private services such as telepurchasing, vocational information, entertainment, and news. Management alternatives range from municipally owned public utilities to nonprofits, from quasi-public consortia to privately owned services.

There are major differences between a prototype information utility and normal commercial development along the lines of greatest profit. These differences, according to Sackman (1972), include:

1. No single organization, public or private, has the skills to develop and manage a mass information utility on a community basis. A broad interdisciplinary team is necessary;

2. The potential for enhancing lifelong education for all citizens for influencing the democratic process is so great that a major public interest is at stake, one that may completely dwarf the immediate commercial interest;

3. Information is a new and unprecedented type of public utility which needs much examination and study for acceptable types of regulation in the public interest;

4. There are many major issues, strategic and tactical, public and private that are likely to arise as the new system evolves, which require special sanctions for the community and a highly flexible management structure for appropriate tests and evaluation;

5. The possibilities of on-line access to public opinion is a major socioeconomic force in its own right, requiring extensive open testing in practice.

Television and radio must be reckoned with as a separate entity within information service utilities. Ellul (1964) has said, "In a world where the human being is unable to make true friendships and to have profound experiences, television and radio furnish him with an appearance of reality, acquaintances, and human proximity." There are no other comparable instruments of human isolation. In a world where the individual really knows very little about his neighbor, the separation between him and his fellows is further widened. There is little face-to-face dialogue.

Television, because of its capacity for auditory and visual penetration, is the most destructive technical instrument of personality and human relations, due to the isolation that grows through its use, despite claims that it brings the world closer together. It is a large world out there, but it is received on a square by one or only a few viewers watching together. The lack of face-to-face confrontation eliminates the opportunity for dialogue and interaction. Of course, there is, in the development of the medium, two-way communication, but it's still *through* the medium and not face-to-face communication.

Consider the video junkie of a not too distant day, snugly ensconced in his all-electric cocoon, lighting up his three-dimensional screen with selections from one hundred channels or the latest purchase from the neighborhood video-disc supermarket. Will this mean the demise of all diversions that require going out? Will anyone tune out long enough to converse with the rest of the family? What about the future of reading or quiet reflecting? Many sociologists believe that this electrical isolation has begun. But this writer believes that this trend can be slowed down or eventually eliminated.

A Possible Next Step

What we have been talking about is the possible collision of technological development with human values. This forces us to make ethical choices, either consciously or subconsciously. The challenge lies in translating values and objectives into action. Values must be linked with direct social actions. They must be integrated into the total planning process, where they are the directional goals and objectives of social development. A leading implication is that philosophers and planners need to know more of each other's trade in order to perform their tasks more effectively. Each of us not only needs to articulate a philosophy based on specific universal values, but also needs to have the skills required for translating values into plans. It is incumbent upon all of us to develop a position and take a stand on our ultimate vision of what technology can and ought to do for society.

The humanities, it seems to me, offer the answer. They must be brought into the dialogue to give perspective and strike a balance between technology and the human condition. How have other civilizations, other cultures handled new ideas, new methods of production, communication, transportation? What have been the results for other civilizations— ethically, morally, socially, and politically—of new technologies? What are the implications for these issues on the proliferation and development of new technology at the present time and in the future?

With future exploration of the humanities, solutions can be suggested, tried, refined, and retried. Educational effort is not enough. It must result in a positive force for change. Misinformation and lack of information have resulted in the current imbalance between technology and the human needs of the public. We have now arrived at the point where we must make a transformation. Decisions must be made in new ways. People must generate the appropriate changes and legislation to really get the job done.

As Harman (1979) has said, "things are too important and too interrelated to leave to the experts. Their perception is too limited by their expertise. It needs the public" (and I would add, the scholars of the humanities) "to put things back in balance." This must be done in a nontechnical way so that the public can understand the issues and their seriousness; raising the public's consciousness is vital. Decision-making is in the hands of the legislatures whose decisions are more and more frequently the result of pressures from special interest groups and individuals. It is time that the special interest groups whose common denominator is the quality of life became a unified force.

Theobald (1981) has said, "We are discovering that all issues are interconnected and that tackling one problem at a time can be profoundly counterproductive." Individual issues are important but it is necessary that all of us become aware of their interconnection. Those who are interested in a more positive future must work together to focus the issues in order to bring about the effective use of modern technology.

For the first time in history, we perceive that everything interacts with everything else; that humankind is confronted with a growing number of global problems; that a unified global society is looming up; and that, for good or evil, it will have a common destiny. In short, a large complex world system is progressively or regressively shaping up or down.

References

Ellul, Jacques, *The Technological Society* (New York: Vantage Books), 1964.

Harman, Willis W., *An Incomplete Guide to the Future* (New York: W.W. Norton & Co.), 1979.

Sackman, Harold, (Ed.), *Planning Community Information Utilities* (Montvale, NJ: AFIPS Press), 1972.

Theobald, Robert, *Beyond Despair: A Policy Guide to the Communications Era* (Washington D.C.: Seven Locks Press, Inc.), 1981.

Bernard G. Kirsch is director of the Institute for Quality Futures, Culver City, California.

3

OPENING THE WORLD OF LEARNING: THE ELECTRONIC CONNECTION

By Bennett H. Berman

Postsecondary institutions in America are locked onto the horns of a double dilemma. Demographically, the aging of America's population, compounded by the trend toward smaller family size, is reducing the number of college-bound students, while conventional classroom instruction and administrative costs keep rising, driving up tuition. Higher tuition further reduces the number of students who can afford to attend and reduces the number of credit hours carried by students per term.

The federal government, the state legislatures, and the taxpaying public have all shown reluctance to approve substantially increased financial support. Fuel has been added to the anti-support fire by research from prestigious sources such as the Carnegie and Ford foundations. They have suggested that the quality of classroom instruction in postsecondary institutions leaves much to be desired. There seems to be a groundswell movement among both students and the public to shift the emphasis in postsecondary instruction from publish-or-perish to teach-and-train.

It is becoming evident that postsecondary institutions of the 1990s will be required to upgrade their instructional progress. They must also "expand" their market through outreach programs if institutions are to survive economically. The trend in expanded outreach can be seen in the establishment of remote campuses, the use of electronic instructional delivery systems, and more adult education.

The growth of the nontraditional, adult learning market in continuing education is well documented. Since continuing education programs needn't clear the hurdles of accreditation, American companies are encouraging their employees to get additional skills training "on their own." Directors of continuing education are in a most advantageous position to generate education for pay. A hypothesis might even be generated that the economic salvation of postsecondary institutions may well depend on the skills of their departments of continuing education as income generating marketers.

Retraining America: Marketing Opportunities

As the timely sands of this century run out, American business, large and small, is looking toward adult education leaders in our postsecondary network for crucial assistance. New technologies from telecommunications to office automation, from computer-integrated manufacturing to electronic data interchange, are affecting every facet of work productivity. Corporate training in America is estimated to cost $40 billion annually. The American Society for Training and Development (ASTD), the leading professional society for private sector training specialists, has tripled in membership from the 1970s to approximately 30,000 members today.

The job of re-educating American workers and managers in the new technologies that affect their productivity and environment is simply too huge for the corporate world to undertake. For example, it can be argued that there are approximately one million jobs in America related directly or indirectly to telecommunications. Spurred by the divestiture of AT&T in a new highly competitive and nonmonopolistic marketplace, the American telecommunications industry has converted in less than five years from an analog signal environment to a digital world where voice and data transmission merge at high speed. At the same time there is a substantial growth occurring in the number of multinational corporations through merger or acquisition who are looking for business development beyond the nation's borders. The planning for an Integrated Service Digital Network (ISDN) is already underway in Europe and Asia. It is being debated currently in America by the Federal Communications Commission. Soon, the world will be electronically linked for voice, data, text, and image transmission in ways never dreamed possible less than a decade ago.

The carriers, manufacturers, interconnect companies, and end users of telecommunications and information technology services must be re-educated to work in this new computerized world. Who is better able to take on a key role in this task than the professional adult education network of American colleges and universities?

The American Association of Community and Junior Colleges' "Keeping America Working" program has attempted to address the issue of jobs lost through technological advancement. The AACJC's "Partners in Progress" videoconference was further evidence of the recognition by both educators and business that they have a common interest: the reeducation of the human infrastructure which supports improved productivity in the workplace.

Distant Learning: Videoconferencing

Among the new technologies that are reshaping the world of communication is videoconferencing via satellites. One of its unique features is its distance insensitivity. In other words, it is virtually as economical to transmit a signal via satellite from New York to Washington as it is from New York to California. The introduction of improvements in antennas and reception equipment has further refined transmission quality.

In 1982 the National University Teleconferencing Network (NUTN) emerged. It delivered special ad hoc events covering a wide range of subjects. At the time of its debut, sixty-seven postsecondary institutions participated, of which only six were equipped to transmit programs (up-links) and only twenty receive sites (downlinks) had permanent equipment installed. During that first year a grand total of ten programs were offered.

Today NUTN has 210 participating colleges and universities. Over 40 of them have permanent uplinks or broadcast capability and more than 100 own permanent receive facilities. In addition, there are now over 100 American corporations with private satellite reception facilities who are notified of NUTN programs and participate on an ad hoc basis.

The National Technological University (NTU) was introduced in 1984 to provide master's and doctoral level degree programs by satellite for engineers. During its initial year courses were provided by twelve partici-pating universities reaching 420 students at sixteen different corporations. By 1987, the student enrollment had swelled to 2,200 with thirty-three universities contributing programs for delivery to sixty-five corporate sites. NTU plans to expand its hi-tech use for offerings in both the accredited and noncredit categories beginning in 1988.

The literature of American education is filled with accounts of single institutions initiating videoconferences and telecourses, computer confer-ences and audiographics (telephone) conferences in efforts to deliver instruc-tion as economically and conveniently as possible. Attempts to evaluate the quality of such instruction tend to suggest that it is certainly as effective, if not more effective, than conventional lecture in the classroom.

Technology Transfer Through Technology Application

Despite the increasing evidence that electronic outreach education is cost-effective and learning-effective, many postsecondary institutions resist investigating the new medium. Facilities at postsecondary institutions reject incorporation of electronic education delivery out of fear of job reduction. Unions in the telecommunications industry and automotive industry have learned the hard way that technological change is as inevitable as the tide or the sunrise. Instead of writing history by adapting to it, too many tradi-tionalists continue to fight history and fall victim to it.

Economic necessity and sociocultural changes will continue to acceler-ate technology transfer into education. Resistance will affect the solvency of the great American educational system, forcing it to seek even more automated technologies for its survival. The alternative is to develop a priv-ileged learning class and surrender the American ideal of education for all. The preferred strategy is to provide the technology transfer needed for America to keep pace with the rest of the world; it is hoped America may even lead the way. Much has been written about the failure of Ameri-can industry to successfully implement the technology it creates. Gener-ally, the success of the Japanese in the world marketplace is attributed to their creative adaptability with technology.

Study after study suggests that American literacy problems are not confined to the inability of some persons to recognize the meaning of visual symbols. The understanding of their meaning is important as well. Learning facts is easy. Using facts is harder. As new technologies and global competition sweep across our nation, it has become evident that while we continue to generate much original research, we tend not to turn that research into practical products or services.

In 1986, the International Center for Information Technologies (ICIT) was created as an independent subsidiary of MCI Telecommunications Corporation. Dr. Peter Keen (1986), ICIT's executive director, is the author of *Competing in Time*, which introduces the premise that those companies who invest in cutting edge technology applications will harvest the reward of their investment within five to seven years. Those companies or organizations which fail to move with technological advances must soon overcome substantial leads of the more aggressive competitors. It is frequently much more costly to play the game of wait-and-see than it is to go out and do.

ICIT was created to serve large public and private sector organizations as a reliable source of information and advise about effective planning, management, and use of information technologies. Its function is to help provide guidance in the interpretation of technology as a tool for improved productivity, performance, or service. It is in this role that ICIT has encouraged consideration of expanded usage of satellite transmitted education on a national and international basis.

The World Community Education Satellite Network

As a service to its members, and to serve the unique interests of the community college population, consideration should be given to the development of a new satellite delivery educational system. This system could target the so-called "blue collar" continuing education student who must acquire new skills to survive in the more complex technical world. This system could provide needed outreach educationally to our "at-risk" population in prisons, hospices, hospitals, and nursing homes. It could even aid dependent children programs. Currently, many women find themselves locked into a child care "prison" without opportunity to gain skills that will enable them to join the roles of the employed.

By linking the United States with other educational networks around the world, it will be possible for a student in Chicago to view and hear an expert on time management strategies from New York on Monday, sit in on a philosophy debate on Wednesday from Oxford University in London, and participate in a dialogue by computer on Friday with an instructor in automotive sciences from Detroit, who was seen on Thursday demonstrating a new electronic engine testing procedure for mechanics. Exploring the use of cutting edge technology in linking members of the educational family is destined to be the thrust of the professional educator worldwide. If America is to retain its position of leadership as a free society in a world without borders, it must actively help to move the theory of electronic education delivery into reality in order to meet the challenges of the Information Age.

References

Berman, Bennett H., "The Economics and Realities of Videoconferencing." A paper presented at The Seventh Annual Teleconference Users Conference (Telecon VII), Disneyland Hotel, Anaheim, CA. November 18, 1987.

Keen, Peter G.W., *Competing In Time: Using Telecommunications for Competitive Advantage* (Cambridge, MA: Ballinger), 1986.

Kelleher, Kathleen and Cross, Thomas B., *Teleconferencing: Linking People Together Electronically* (Englewood, NJ: Prentice Hall, Inc.), 1985.

Martin, James, *Telematic Society: A Challenge for Tomorrow* (Englewood Cliffs, NJ: Prentice-Hall, Inc.), 1981.

Parker, Lorne A. and Olgren, Christine H. (eds.), *Teleconferencing and Electronic Communication IV,* (Madison, Wis.: Center for Interactive Programs, University of Wisconsin), 1985.

Bennett H. Berman is dean of educational services, International Center for Information Technologies, Washington, D.C.

Toward Telecommunity College: from Open Admissions to Open Learning

.

By Seymour Eskow

Woody Allen's "Radio Days," another of his unique mixtures of slapstick and sociology, reminds us of radio's power when it first arrived: how it changed the nature of work and politics in our nation, the structure of our family life, how it altered the very fabric of the American psyche. What radio did not change, of course, was the American college.

Older colleagues who lived through those first radio days, and younger colleagues who know the history of educational technology in America, remember the hopes for radio, the predictions, and the wave of experiments. Radio was to dissolve the barriers of space and time and cost that had previously limited educational opportunity. It would bring the best minds of Harvard and The Sorbonne to the small towns and small colleges of America; the best music, the best poetry (read by T.S. Eliot and W.B. Yeats) would be in our dormitories, our homes, and our curricula; and the curriculum committee would reshape the study of the arts and sciences so that they would embrace the literature, the history, the sociology created by radio.

One might consider that the ability of radio to deliver on those early promises is still there; if the colleges of the United States wanted to harness that power, radio could be used to create a learning network of great value. However, such a learning network will not be created, and if educational radio were to disappear tomorrow, most professors and students would not know that it was gone.

Is there any point in rehearsing the radio days, the television days, all of the failed utopias of yesterday? Of course. We continue to teach history in our colleges because we believe that yesterday is the only compass and map that we have to chart our course today, and to predict where we will be tomorrow. Indeed, we deliver Santayana's warning to our students: who does not know history is doomed to repeat it. If we do not remember the radio days, we will repeat them as computer days.

Our sense of the past becomes our guide to the future; yesterday's scenario becomes our script for tomorrow.

I suggest that those who believe in the power of the new technologies to transform education have a view of the past that has become their folklore and conventional wisdom—and their guide to the future. After a brief sketch of that interpretation of yesterday, I suggest another: our view of the past leads to other proposals for the future. Some of them are outlined here.

Radio Days: The Conventional Wisdom

There are at least two versions of the standard script. The first, and by far the most common in the literature of academic innovation, argues that our colleges are in the grip of a professoriate determined to maintain its domain and dominance, unwilling to consider seriously any changes that depart from those styles of teaching and learning common in the Middle Ages: the professor as actor performing before students as auditors and audience. The professors have used their control over the curriculum and the methods of instruction that have a pedagogical power far beyond that of the lecture, the text, and the chalkboard. Supporting and extending the power of the professors are the external agencies that monitor, regulate, and finance education: the accrediting agencies, the licensure boards, the state departments of public instruction—bodies that refuse to accredit or license or fund instruction unless it is delivered by a professor in a classroom on a campus, denying to uncounted students the teaching power of the new technologies.

There you have the basic script. Typically, it is embellished with personal accounts of dreams and schemes foiled by the English department or the curriculum council or the faculty senate. What reformer does not have stories to tell? (One thinks of the hero in Stringfellow Barr's *Purely Academic,* who spent every other year trying to persuade the curriculum committee to change the curriculum and the alternate year in drinking.)

Another version of the script locates the resistance to change not in the professoriate, but in the intellectual technology that has been the organizing principle of the American college at least since Charles Eliot's time. That technology is perhaps best summarized and symbolized by the schedule of courses and classes that come about after "registration:" higher education as five courses of fifty minutes each, each offered three times a week for three "credits." The schedule embodies all of the ways in which the higher learning is organized in the United States: knowledge organized into "departments" as well as disciplines, each with its own department head; an elaborate system of academic accountancy grounded in the fiction that an education can be pieced together from interchangeable parts; a system, as has been often pointed out, that shares much of the culture of the factory and the assembly line. The language and style of the factory color such a system: the buildings on campus are the "plant," students are "personnel" or sometimes "raw material," and learning is a "product" that can be produced, controlled, and measured with the tools of engineering.

It is this tightly organized and coherent system, then, that resists any change that is not congenial, that threatens to disrupt the orderly flow of work and the distribution of roles and rewards. And it is not only changes in the academic style proposed by the supporters of educational technology that are not welcomed; such purely conceptual changes as independent study, learning contracts, credit by examination, or service learning, which require no radios or computers, are also not compatible with the system and are not widely embraced and endorsed.

While the two scenarios have much in common, their differences are significant for reformers who would bring computers to the campus. Those who locate the resistance in the professors believe that appeals, persuasion, and programs of faculty education can change the nature of college instruction. The other view sees the professors as part of a complex technology that is maintained and controlled by forces within and without the academy.

Newman's Idea: The College As Community

In one version of yesterday, then, it is the professors, fearing for their power or their jobs, who have kept the new tools of learning away from the campus. In another, it is the system of teaching and learning designed by the professors that rejects any new pedagogy that does not fit easily into the old system.

We propose here another version of history, one that casts the actors differently, and one that points to a different future for the campus and for the new technology.

In "Sign of the Times," a prescient essay written in 1831, Carlyle demonstrated that "the mechanical principle" was invading every sphere of life, that the logic and the style of the factory were reshaping all of the world's institutions and relations. The college and university were not exempt; they too would be reformed by the mechanical principle.

It was against those who applauded the reshaping of the university to conform to the spirit of an industrial age, including Carlyle himself, who believed that the university of the future would be a collection of books, that Newman (1938) upheld the older vision. A university, he said, "is a place for the communication and circulation of thought, by means of personal intercourse." There were other important ways to learn: skills and recipes from books, manners from the court, style from the city; and Newman would make all of these ways of learning widely available to those who preferred them or had no choice:

> such certainly is our popular education, and its effects are remarkable. Nevertheless, after all, even in this age, whenever men are really serious. . .when they aim at something precise, something refined, something really luminous. . .they avail themselves, in some shape or other, of the rival method, the ancient method, of oral instruction. . .between man and man, of teachers instead of learning, of the personal influence of a master, and the humble initiation of a discipline (Newman 1938, p. 32).

Some of our professors may indeed be Luddites, resisting machines because their jobs are threatened. More, we think, share the Newmanian vision of the campus as community, as a place where teachers and students come together to talk, to work, and to learn. The mechanical principle has already disrupted that community: the fragmenting of the curriculum and the organization of the schedule disconnect teachers from students and students from each other. Radio, television sets, and computers on campus threaten to finish the work of anticommunity: each student in a carrel, with earphones, watching images and words on a screen, listening to disembodied voices, pushing buttons quietly.

The overriding question, then, for those who believe in the liberating power of the new technology, is this: what is the vision of the campus of the future, and how does that campus adapt to and harness the new technology?

Our own answer is this. The campus of the future will be a place where men and women come together to learn together. Discussion and dialogue-talk will be the way learning is carried on. There will be rooms, halls, and buildings designed to support and encourage many conversations. Surrounding these central buildings will be libraries, bookstores, and centers with radios, television sets, and computers, and men and women will move easily from the places of conversation to these stores and centers in search of books, speech, and images as they explore matters of concern to them, or in search of the kind of tutoring and drill and practice that machines can provide.

Most of our students of the future will not, however, use the new technology on campus. They will have learning centers with computers and videotape and interactive videodisc players in their homes and in their workplaces, so that they can do independent research, be tutored, sharpen their skills, or learn new ones at home, at work, or in hotel rooms when they travel. Most important, the computer will allow them to communicate with their teachers for personal tutoring and to share ideas with fellow students through electronic classrooms, so that teachers and students dispersed in time and space are still collaborating in the work of learning.

The design of the college of the future as I see it, then, has oral community at its center, and technology at its borders and dispersed throughout the community, so that teachers and students talk together on campus and use the new technology to create new kinds of learning communities that are not grounded in time and place. We call that college of the future "Telecommunity College." What follows are notes for an agenda of issues and concerns raised by such a view of the future.

The New Community College: Forces and Influences

1. From an Intentional Community for Youth to a Lifespan College.

The forms of the American college—and all the world's colleges—were shaped by their mission as communities for the instruction

28

of youth. The new college is a place for all of the adults of the community, and this new commitment will change the look of the campus, the relations between teachers and students, and the styles of communication and instruction.

The classic college was a total institution, with its own living quarters, entertainment, and community services; the gown did not need the town. The lifespan college will be a learning community, sharing its students with churches, employers, and human service agencies and collaborating with those agencies in the design of learning.

2. Open Admission and Open Learning

The image of the "open door college" is the self-image of the community college: the image of a house of learning opening its doors to receive new guests. Adults need to learn in many other settings: in their homes, their churches, their places of business. The new community college will open the door outward, so that teachers, students, and learning can move out from the college and into the community. The new community college will be a richer learning environment; it will also end the notion that learning takes place only on a campus in groups of thirty under the watchful eye of the professor.

- *Open admission.* The door opens in. *Open learning.* The door opens out.

- *Open learning.* A student with a learning contract studying at home, in the community, anywhere in the world. He or she has a mentor back on campus, finds books and colleagues, learns in and from the world: travel, work, service, the action curriculum.

- *Open learning.* A student at a computer, at home, at work, traveling, in a hospital, prison, in an army barracks. The student types an essay, asks a question, hits a key and sends the essay and the question to an electronic mailbox. A professor at a computer, reading an essay, noting the question. The professor types comments on the essay, answers the question, assigns new work, hits a key and the words are sent to the student. (Question: is this exchange more or less personal than sitting in a class of thirty? Is the technology dehumanizing teaching and learning or restoring the tutorial role of the teacher?)

- *Open learning.* The external degree. The British had a long tradition of external degrees before Open University. Thomas Edison College, Regents College, and a handful of American colleges and universities offer external degrees. How many community colleges have done away with residency requirements and offer external degrees? (Residency requirements restrict student mobility and do not create community.)

3. Three Partners

- *The idea of teaching partnerships.* Some of the best teaching and learning results when we partner, formally or implicitly, with noncollege agencies. The teaching hospital: a compact between the agency and the college to work together to train future doctors and nurses: cooperative education. The longstanding partnership with textbook publishers: those provide dollars and expertise and create learning materials while colleges provide the store on the campus and help them sell those materials to the students. Cultural programs on campus often are designed with, and income shared with, talent bureaus and booking agencies. The new community college, the lifespan college, needs the collaboration of three sectors of society.

- *The colleges.* To create the campus as a place of assembly; to bring together libraries, laboratories, and other tools of learning; to provide the credentialing structure; to house the teaching faculty; to provide the links between the faculty and other agencies of the community.

- *The agencies and institutions of the community.* The home, so that the homes of the community become learning places, extensions of the campus: perhaps the real residency requirement is that the student be able and willing to study at home. The computer and modem allow the man or woman with child care responsibilities to have personal tutoring without leaving the home; the elderly, the incapacitated, can take part in learning, earn credits and degrees, learn new skills. The hospital as part of the campus. The prison, the military base. The church. The workplace: the factory, the office, the store equipped with computers, tape and disc players, the telephones become places of learning linked to teachers, libraries, information. We have telemarketing, telecommuting. Why not *telelearning?*

- *The learning businesses.* Since the learning community on campus is primarily a face-to-face community, we do not need many tools: the book and the blackboard. To move ideas, knowledge, and skills into homes and workplaces will require that we partner with those who own and manage telephone networks, create software, and design learning systems incorporating several communication technologies. They are eager to work with us, and will if we understand and accept the principles that motivate the private sector. And of course they will have to understand and respect the values and the culture of college.

If the colleges can learn to link their resources and skills with those of the other agencies of society and those of the learning businesses, they will invent adult learning systems we cannot now imagine, ways of learning appropriate for a society that must view lifetime learning as its ultimate resource.

4. Networks: Horizontal and Vertical

• *The Community Network.* The college as part of, creator of, the learning web of each community, linking, in the ecology of learning, with the other adult agencies concerned with the welfare of the people of the community.

• *The State Network.* Consider a state with thirty community colleges and a commitment to economic development. How do the community colleges work with the employers of the state that have branches in many parts of the state? With government agencies that want to move programs of information to all the employers of the state? With human service agencies, cultural agencies, churches, and other institutions that have statewide, and larger, commitments?

The community colleges pride themselves, rightly, on their commitment to local community service. Increasingly, they are seeing themselves as a state network, willing to negotiate as a single, decentralized educational system to meet statewide needs. To do this means granting new powers to state agencies concerned with the coordination of community college systems or creating some other mechanism for negotiating with statewide employers and others on behalf of all the colleges.

Suppose the 106 community colleges of California were connected to each other by computer and modem as well as to their local industries and homes, and suppose the colleges were willing to harness those computers for instruction. If this were done, every industry and every home in the state would have access to all the curricula and all the faculty talents of the state. Each college would offer its own core studies in general and liberal studies, and such business and technical curricula that must be available locally. The specialized courses and curricula requiring scarce faculty talents would not need to be duplicated, but could be sent out over the telephone lines or by satellite to any firm, agency, or home in the state.

• *The National Network.* America is a nation of voluntary associations serving the interests and needs of their members. Many, perhaps most, of these assume some responsibility for the continuing education of their members. Can we join forces with professional associations, for example, in creating and implementing their programs of continuing education? Can we serve as the training agency for the businesses and industries that have a national presence? Who calls on General Electric or The Aetna on behalf of all the community colleges of the nation? Is this the proper sale of the American Association of Community and Junior Colleges, or the Association of Community College Trustees?

There are very few places in the United States that cannot now be reached by telephone, cable, or satellite. Connected to each other and using the new technologies to move learning, the colleges can move the old ideal of equal access to the next level of possibility.

- *International Networks.* In the last twenty years the community colleges have come to agree that localism is not provincialism, that each community in the United States depends for its security and work on the state of the world. Perhaps three hundred community colleges of the nation now help students spend one or more semesters in another country and culture. (There is work to be done here: some states still require that courses be taught by state-certified teachers, so that instruction offered by Oxford dons cannot be recognized.)

The world is increasingly wired together, with copper wire and fiber optics, with uplinks and downlinks. Instruction can move easily from the United States to Japan or Colombia or England or the U.S.S.R., to our students in those countries, or to students from those countries who choose to become our students. And, of course, instruction originating in those countries can move to the United States and to our students who want to learn about other countries and cultures.

International Telecommunity College needs no new technology, no great fundraising effort. The infrastructure is in place. All that is required is imagination, organization, and will.

Designing the New Community College

The diffusion of knowledge. Thomas Jefferson, Benjamin Franklin, and most of the founding fathers were interested in the distinction between instruction that went on in schools and colleges, and the diffusion of knowledge, which used agencies like the Junto, the subscription library, the town meeting, and the free press. The new community college will create a rich academic community and will take responsibility for the diffusion of knowledge, using the newer technologies as well as the classic forms of extension and dissemination.

The Community College as the New Chautauqua. The Chautauqua movement, once the largest and best known adult education enterprise in the world, was a place—the institution in western New York state that still flourishes as a learning community—and a circuit of culture tent shows created by entrepreneurs that moved lectures, drama, debate, and entertainment to the remote places of the United States. The Chautauqua Literary and Scientific Circles were study circles that once involved hundreds of thousands of people around the world in reading and discussion. Chautauqua, then, was both a place where people came to learn and a force that moved learning around the nation and the world.

The *place* Chautauqua might be the form the new community college campus should take. It is not a campus but a community with housing of every kind, stores, and all the services and amenities of a community, and threaded throughout the community are places designed for learning: the amphitheater, small buildings for study and discussion, a library, a bookstore. One gets up in the morning and decides whether to attend a lecture or go to the library or go boating or visit friends or take a class; learning blends into the other activities of adult life. While activities are scheduled and announced, they are not packaged in fifty-minute segments; each is designed according to its own logic, and adults decide whether they want to spend an hour or a day or weeks on a particular learning venture. There is a resident symphony orchestra, theater company, and many visiting performers and lecturers. The community college might be such a place; there could be smaller centers in neighborhoods, in churches, in workplaces, and in hospitals, all drawing on the resources of the college.

(Thoreau proposed, in *Walden*, that every community become a university. Although he was a Harvard graduate and used the Harvard library throughout his life, he did not use Harvard as his model for the community university, but the Concord Lyceum.)

Telecommunity College. For those in the community who cannot come to the place of learning, or who choose not to come, the new community college will help create such places in their homes, workplaces, or institutions.

The distinction between high tech and high touch is misleading. The telephone, high tech, allows one to touch children, parents, friends; without it, one would touch them only by letter, also a form of technology, and without the technology of mail one would have almost no way of reaching those cared about. The media of communication allow touching those one cannot otherwise reach.

Telecommunity. We no longer must be near each other to establish human communities of mutuality and concern. The computer-mediated conference allows the forming of a community of common interest with people never seen, in one's own town, throughout the nation, around the world.

The community college changed the face of American postsecondary education after World War II with this bold assertion: everyone could learn and should have access to learning. The logic and rhetoric of the community college movement is now more than forty years old, and much has happened since the first announcement of the vocabulary of open door and equal access, and terminal and transfer curricula.

The new technology might allow our campuses to be made more humane places of learning for adults. And it might allow fulfillment of the old pledges in new ways, by circulating and communicating data, information, knowledge, and wisdom to everyone who wants them.

We can invent Telecommunity College.

Reference

Newman, John Henry, "The Idea of a University" in *Essays English and American* (New York: Collier), 1938.

Seymour Eskow is president of The Electronic University Network, San Francisco, California.

5

LEADERSHIP FOR A
LEARNING SOCIETY

.

By Ervin L. Harlacher

As we approach the 21st century, the evolution and implementation of new technologies and the dramatic changes in demographic, social, and work patterns will require us to rethink basic operational concepts of the community college, most of which are products of the Industrial Revolution. One of these reconsiderations is the concept of executive leadership.

The future, however, is shaped by the present and the past; the scenario for the twenty-first century is being written today. Trends associated with the information society are shaping the learning society of tomorrow and will have a major impact on the community college in the twenty-first century (Naisbitt, 1982, Toffler, 1983, and Naisbitt and Aburdeen, 1985). These trends include

- An acceleration of job obsolescence and a redefinition of jobs that remain;
- The emergence of training and retraining as an integral part of every worker's lifetime;
- The replacement of the standardization of the industrial age with multiple options and individual choice;
- Several careers in a worker's lifetime;
- The replacement of the "linear life plan" of the industrial society with a "blended life plan" which emphasizes lifespan learning;
- A dramatic shift in the number of employed women and minorities;
- A shrinking of the work week to an average of 25 hours by the year 2000; and
- A gradual greying of the American population.

Our rapid shift from the "muscle power" economy of the Industrial Revolution to the "knowledge-based" economy of the information society will affect the nature and structure of the community college, demanding more from executive leadership than ever before. Yet, according to Roueche, Baker, and Rose (1988), Warren Bennis and Burt Nanus in 1985 cited a crisis of executive leadership in America's institutions, concluding that "if there was ever a moment in history when a comprehensive strategic view of leadership was needed, not by just a few leaders in high office but by large numbers of leaders in every job, this is certainly it" (p. 49).

Many of the current generation of executive leaders have not been equipped by experience or training to respond effectively to the challenges of the information society. This crisis of executive leadership is also critical in the community college. Roueche, Baker, and Rose (1988) have reasoned that "...the relative newness of these organizations and the constant criticism by those who believe that their colleges are incapable of delivering what they have promised have led to a crisis of confidence in the movement" (p. 49).

The challenges of the 21st century, just a decade away, must be faced by a new, visionary breed of executive leader. Accordingly, the selection and preparation of community college executive leaders becomes one of our highest priorities. Above all, the new generation of executive leaders must (1) be prepared to fully utilize technology in a cost-effective manner, and (2) possess the vision of a learning society that transcends institutional goals and serves the broader lifespan learning needs of the community as a whole.

Change, accelerated by technological development, is affecting individuals and organizations at a rate never before experienced in the history of mankind (Naisbitt and Aburdene 1985). Joel Goldhar observed in 1984 that "product life cycles are getting shorter. Every industry we look at seems to be undergoing shorter cycles. For example, "the micro computer, now in wide spread use, was virtually unheard of seven years ago. The refrigerator, in contrast, took more than 30 years to develop" (Cetron 1984, p. 25).

America is fast becoming a learning society. Knowledge—a primary lever of all societies—is the "new wealth" of the information society, increasing the importance of education. Yet, Naisbitt and Aburdene (1985) report that adults entering the work force are less skilled than ever before. They consider unskilled workers the major obstacle to prosperity in an information society, attributing the problem to an educational system essentially unchanged since the Industrial Revolution. The community college is the logical institution to meet this challenge and spread the "new wealth" among the people.

The future of the community college will be significantly affected by our success or failure in meeting the unprecedented technological and societal challenges of the twenty-first century. History has taught us that institutions that fail to serve society's needs and interests are cast aside so that something else can evolve from the vacuum created. An effective response, however, can make the community college the center of most Americans' lives in the 21st century.

Genesis of Modern Leadership

Nothing in the pursuit of excellence is more important than studying models of things that work. Therefore, education has begun to look to government, the military, and business and industry for executive leadership models, even though researchers have admitted that differences exist. Writers have also pointed out that executive leadership is exercised somewhat differently in the private sector than in the public sector and still differently in the civic sector. And there is a striking difference between what is done by appointed executives in government and elected executive leaders, who are generally considered less legitimate (Cunningham 1985).

What is leadership? Leadership has been considered as "almost nothing" and "almost everything." Some researchers insist that there is little empirical evidence to suggest that personal leadership makes a difference in organizational outcomes, characterizing the chief executive officer as the "driver of a skidding car," or a "light bulb in a dark room," with the conclusion that it makes little difference whether he or she is a 100 or 300 watt CEO (Birnbaum 1988, p. 145). Other researchers have found that personalized leadership is desired by all organizations, and that associated with almost every successful organization is a strong leader (Peters and Austin, 1987).

The concept of leadership has been studied for generations by biographers, historians, and social scientists of all stripes, yielding a multitude of definitions, theories, and models. Since the 1920s, leadership has been defined functionally as an *influencing* process: an active and strategic skill that involves influencing the behavior of others toward goals (Niehouse, 1987). Leadership is the catalyst that helps organizations forge ahead in the face of adversity, to challenge the norm, and to inspire great performance from their people.

Most writers today distinguish between leadership and management. "Managers are people who do things right and leaders are people who do the right thing" (Bennis and Nanus, 1985, p. 21). Leaders, however, are not absolved from performing management tasks. The more successful leaders are assumed to have mastered the state-of-the-art management skills, including most of the traditional functions that begin with planning and end with evaluating, and the techniques of decision making, communications, and advocacy. The office of the college president, in fact, while declining in significance, is seen as becoming more and more managerial (Benezet, Katz, and Magnusson, 1981).

Leaders as managers must make sure that their executive subordinates make maximum use of the potential development of the organization's capital, human skills, raw material, and technology. Management, according to Roueche, Baker, and Rose (1988), is the ability to integrate human skills with technology—such as policies, procedures, systems, and equipment—for the purpose of organizing those elements necessary to accomplish the college's mission and purpose. These same authors view leadership, on the other hand, as more concerned with influencing human behavior.

Students of leadership have chipped away at the concept of leadership by offering various explanations of (1) what attributes or qualities leaders possess, (2) what leaders do, and (3) how leaders behave in different situations. These approaches are consistent with the three distinct periods through which leadership theory has evolved: the trait, behavioral, and situational/contingency periods.

Trait Period. The earliest approach was the trait or great man theory, which posits "that leaders are persons endowed with specific physical, personality, or ability traits to a greater extent than non-leaders" (Birnbaum, 1988, p. 136). Prior to the mid-1800s leadership theory was primarily concerned with determining those traits "which distinguish leaders from non-leaders or followers . . . or separate 'great leaders' from the masses. . . ." (Flowers 1985, p. 4). While there are numerous examples of the trait approach in the literature, one of the most recent is George Vaughan's *The Community College Presidency* (1986).

Writers in the field have identified traits that contribute to leader "personality." Leadership is not shortness or tallness, not sweetness nor harshness. Such traits are seldom predictors of success or failure. Leadership is something else: charisma, self-esteem, dedication, predictability, inspiration, high motivation, passion, and loyalty.

John W. Gardner has identified fourteen attributes of leadership: physical vitality and stamina (which he suggests is one of the few ingredients essential to leadership that can't be learned); intelligence and judgment-in-action; willingness and eagerness to accept responsibility; knowledge of the task at hand; understanding of followers/constituents and their needs; skill in dealing with people; need to achieve; capacity to motivate; courage, resolution, and steadiness; capacity to win and hold trust; capacity to manage, decide, and set priorities; confidence; ascendance, dominance, and assertiveness; and adaptability or flexibility of approach *(Los Angeles Times* August 17, 1987).

Bennis (1985) has suggested that successful leaders share traits similar to those of explorers. They are enthusiastic and energizing, perceptive and empathetic, analytic, curious, considerate, self-reliant, persistent, intuitive, and caring and nurturing. They follow up on obvious things that other people have missed; are unceasing in their quest for information, always asking questions and seeking truths; use common sense; have the ability to take complex ideas and present them in simple ways, often painting word pictures; trust their *gut* instincts; are willing to take risks, even if they make mistakes, because they realize that failure is no reason to get discouraged; and are decisive—they consider alternatives and pick a direction and move forward, but demand the right to change.

Successful leaders also are aware of their personal priorities; are positive, realizing that disaster is no reason to get discouraged; are conscientious, fostering loyalty in their younger subordinates; are sensitive to other people's hopes, dreams, and aspirations and know how to translate them into reality; have historical perspective; and supergeneralists who can assimilate, integrate, and act on the vast and diverse array of information available; are goal-oriented and enjoy helping shape events and things;

and have the ability to get things done, with good organization abilities and productive work habits.

Joseph (1984) has added four additional traits or basic skills to those offered by other writers: first, thinking, which he suggests no one teaches; second, opportunity finding, finding opportunities in change, not just problem solving; third, cognitive skills to make our minds more effective; and fourth, global thinking, thinking about the world as one big market.

Finally, in discussing the management of change, Bennis and Nanus (1985) identified five additional traits:

1. Foresight, in order to judge how the vision fits into the way the environment of the organization may evolve;
2. Hindsight, in order that the vision does not violate the traditions and culture of the organization;
3. Depth perception, in order to see the whole picture in detail and perspective;
4. Peripheral vision, so that the effect of the new direction on competitors and other stakeholders can be understood;
5. A process of revision, so that all visions are continuously reviewed as the environment changes (p. 102).

In another recent study, Duncan (1988) identified several additional leadership traits in the literature, most of which she later validated in field interviews. She classified the traits under five clusters: intrapersonal, interpersonal, ethical/moral, intellectual, and physical.

The intrapersonal cluster included such additional traits as sense of humor, drive and ambition, persistence, optimism, resourcefulness, discretion, and patience and prudence. Added to the list from the personal interviews were self-confidence, action-oriented, dependability, direction, impatience to achieve, tolerance for frustration, consistency, and outgoing demeanor.

Identified in the literature under the interpersonal cluster were such additional traits as compassion and articulation. The field interviews added consensus builder, persuasiveness, friendliness, tactfulness, straightforwardness, and eloquence.

All of the traits under the ethical/moral cluster were identified in field interviews: moral code; fairness; evangelism; having good character; trustworthiness; and honesty, forthrightness, and integrity.

The literature revealed four additional traits under the intellectual cluster: open and inquisitive mind; initiative; wisdom; and intuitive thinker. Added during the field interviews were sharing of ideas, retentive memory, sharing of credit for successes, farsightedness, creativity, innovation, and seeking excellence for self and others.

Finally, one additional trait, high energy, was identified by Duncan in the literature under the physical cluster. And visibility—omnipresence—was added during the interviews.

Behavioral Period. The second approach considered not what leaders *are,* but what leaders *do* and how they *behave.* Duncan's 1988 research determined that successful leaders perform the roles of visionary, communicator, collaborator, change agent, risk taker, servant, teacher, life-long learner, role model, social architect, and politician. Other writers in the field have added coach, guide, enabler, counselor, cheerleader, entrepreneur, power broker, manager, "genetic designer, engineer of a living thing; inspirer and preacher; high priest and mystic; and artist and creator" (Raymond, 1986).

Leader behavior is linked to subordinate satisfaction and performance in the behavioral paradigm. Similar to the trait theory, an attempt was made to determine a universal leadership behavioral pattern by which the researcher can assess leadership effectiveness (Flowers, 1985). (According to Hershey and Blanchard [1986], behavioral theory has its roots in two extreme schools of management thought: scientific management and human relations.)

While delivering the Harry S. Truman Lecture in 1987, John Gardner suggested nine behaviors or tasks performed by executive leaders: envisioning goals, affirming values, motivating, managing, explaining, achieving a workable level of unity, serving as a symbol, representing the group externally, and renewing (Gardner, 1987).

Other writers have determined that successful leaders also build consensus and team spirit; engage in critical thinking; use appropriate strategies for decision making and negotiations; communicate openly and listen actively to others; accept risks, viewing mistakes and failures as learning experiences; and establish standards, expectations, and norms.

Most of the leadership behaviors listed above were also cited by Duncan (1988). Through subsequent field interviews she also determined that successful CEOs do the following: identify themselves with institutional excellence; keep their institution on the "cutting edge of technology" in management; present a strong public presence; direct their institution by asking strategic questions; follow through on decisions; negotiate skillfully; and survive by knowing zones of acceptance.

Situational/Contingency Period. Since the 1960s, the situational/contingency paradigm has been a dominant approach among leadership researchers. This approach considers the personality and maturity of the followers: leadership is viewed as a dynamic process involving leaders, followers, leader-follower relationships, leader roles, and other situational variables. "Every part is connected to every other part, and every decision affects every other decision" (Walker, 1979, p. 102). Commenting on the dynamics of the process, Campbell (1970) notes that the tasks of situational leaders differ substantially one from another and that the work of a particular leader reflects individual characteristics, situational variables, and organizational contexts.

The early research during this period was done by Fiedler. It focused on the personalities of the leader and the group, and the nature of the situation; the leader was considered effective if the group did well (Fiedler, 1967).

Prior to the work of Hershey and Blanchard (1977), leadership style was generally equated with two extremes, authoritarian (directive) and democratic (supportive). Their research, however, focused on the "maturity level of the followers" in the leadership relationship, indicating that different maturity levels required different combinations of directive and supportive behaviors. Four basic leadership styles, representing different combinations of directive and supportive behavior, were identified by Hershey and Blanchard: supporting, delegating, coaching, and directing. These four styles are used flexibly and interchangeably, depending upon the situation, skills, and commitment of the followers. All of these factors can vary from situation to situation, resulting in a mind-boggling number of possible scenarios.

No single leadership style is the best; however, the leader's dominant style may influence our perception of the organization as being bureaucratic, collegial, or political. Successful leaders have the ability to diagnose the situation, reach agreements with their people about their needs, and adapt their leadership style accordingly; they recognize that different situations require different responses. Situational leaders are effective in interacting with different types of people, because they make an effort to understand the differences in people's behaviors and styles.

Furthermore, not all approaches are equally effective in every situation. Writers in the field have described the leadership style of successful leaders as "aggressive opportunism," and "an astonishing combination of direction and empowerment." Others have added that successful leaders are "tough and tender, patient and insistent, rigid and flexible. They use theories 'X' and 'Y' simultaneously" (Waterman, 1987 and Peters, 1985).

Characteristics of Successful Leaders

Effective leadership, according to Diebold (1984), has the appearance of being effortless, even superfluous. "A leader is one who, when the battle is won, leaves behind the conviction that the people did it themselves," he adds, quoting a Chinese proverb which he believes is still appropriate today (p. 400).

Successful executive leaders are powerful men and women who are results-oriented; they make what they believe in happen—they stamp their organizations in a special way, leaving distinctive imprints—a lasting legacy of their individuality. To the extent that they enable their followers to develop their own initiative, these executive leaders create something that can survive their own departure (Gardner, 1987).

What does it take to be a successful executive leader? First, recognition that the most valuable resource is the human resource. Successful executive leaders are characterized by a high degree of sensitivity toward others; they view their staff as persons of individual worth and independent rights, who, if given the chance, provided the vision is clear and unchanging, will contribute to the common good. Peter Drucker concluded in 1954 that decisive change, the foundation of organizational revitalization, occurs when the employee "... is valued as a vital resource, not a mere cost center" (Bennis 1985, p. 26). When people are treated as the main engine rather than interchangeable parts of the corporate machine, motivation, creativity, quality, and commitment to implementation well up (Waterman, 1987).

Second, recognition that creativity is the critical stuff of leadership. Leaders are creative men and women of vision who have set their sights high and believe in the power of dreams. Sometimes we think too small, like the frog in the old Chinese story. Sitting at the bottom of a well, it thinks the sky is only as big as the opening at the top of the well. Creative leaders innovate by combining useful old and new ideas to open up new possibilities and solve problems, rather than treat symptoms.

Third, recognition that the executive leader's own personal philosophy and standards of professional conduct, including ethics and morals, are perceived to be the foundation for the organization's value system. Successful executive leadership is built upon an ethical and moral foundation, mutually subscribed to by leader and followers. We hold our leaders to higher standards in their exercise of power; we expect them to be sensitive to ethical and moral issues; demonstrate integrity and fairness; know right from wrong and be honest, trustworthy, and forthright; and be responsible and accountable. Burns (1978) defined leadership in its purest sense as a process of morality where leaders are engaged with followers on the basis of shared motives, values, and goals.

Fourth, recognition that there is a fundamental difference between management by commitment and command. While freedom and respect for the individual are great motivators, commitment and ownership are two of the most important words in the English language when the issue is motivation and productivity. According to Waterman (1987), commitment results from grand causes which permit people throughout the organization to contribute to the central purpose. Commitment fosters initiative, entrepreneurship, risk taking, creativity, and the investment of extra effort, according to Fryer (1988). "The goal of eliciting high levels of commitment from those who perform the work of the enterprise," Fryer added, "is the animating value of a theory of ideal governance for community colleges."

Fifth, recognition that "the management of meaning, mastery of communication, is inseparable from effective leadership" (Bennis and Nanus, 1985, p. 33). Several writers have reported that the successful executive leaders they studied were unceasing in their quest for information, had well developed oral and written communication skills, and were formidable in distributing information. They were expressive and fluent public speakers and "adroit deployers of moral suasion," as evidenced by an unusual ability to inform and persuade; were superior in maintaining an open and active two-way communication system, which encouraged a free flow of information throughout the organization; and had the ability to communicate effectively with people at all levels of the organization. But as every community college president knows instinctively, communicating within the college is only half the battle. Dialogue must also be maintained with the college's external constituents. If anything, experienced leaders err in favor of over-communicating.

Successful executive leaders also know how to listen carefully to all of their constituents, and have developed innovative approaches to "active listening." One is "managing by walking around" (stopping to talk with others in their offices). A second approach, "naive listening," requires leaders to work in line jobs to learn directly about the needs of their employees and customers. Both of these approaches acknowledge that our expertise as leaders may prevent us from listening effectively and being responsive (Peters and Waterman, 1982 and Peters and Austin, 1985).

Several writers have suggested that the new breed of executive leader required to revitalize America is the "transformational leader," defined by Burns (1978) as one who provides a vision while helping the organization work through the process of revitalization; one who induces followers to achieve goals that represent that vision; the values and the motivations of both the leader (and therefore the organization) and the followers; one who empowers others to perform by pulling rather than pushing, challenging rather than manipulating, and encouraging rather than controlling. Transformational leaders are not only able to envision the future clearly, but are also able to communicate that vision to others and inspire them to commit to it themselves.

Leadership is no longer preoccupied with just making decisions. Successful executive leaders are sensitive people who are willing to take risks; to set the vision and inspire a following; to persist and persevere, taking advantage of opportunities as they arise; to empower others to higher levels of performance; to make everyone a hero; and to stand against the status quo for the betterment of the organization.

Conclusion

The emerging information society, with its emphasis on technology and lifespan learning, will have a profound effect on the community college of the twenty-first century. Learning has already become a lifespan necessity for almost everyone. A clear acknowledgment of this fact was the adoption of a lifelong learning policy by the U.S. Department of Education.

Knowledge is the "new wealth" of the learning society. It gives people the means to work more efficiently. According to Joseph (1984), "that means that eventually it takes fewer people to do the same amount of work. As a result," he continued, "people get displaced from jobs and need retraining, reeducating or, at the minimum a supported reentry period" (p. 133). Current knowledge, skills, and competencies have become the ticket to participation in that society for individuals and groups. Jobs, the economy, and life styles will be increasingly based on the creation and distribution of information.

No job which now exists, according to Joseph (1984), will not be in jeopardy by the year 2000; new jobs and changed jobs will mean training, lots of training. (Presently many workers must be retrained three to four times during their careers.) For the next 20 years many occupations may become so transient that complete retraining will be required every four to five years. "We are going to be re-careering" throughout our lives, Joseph concluded (p. 135).

"Future generations. . .must be educated for life in an increasingly complex world. . .," as pointed out by the Commission on the Future of Community Colleges (American Association of Community and Junior Colleges, 1988, p. 49). The supply of knowledge and information will not be the problem, but rather its effective selection and delivery. The community college is the most appropriate institution to assist *most* Americans with this critical selection and delivery problem. We now have the means to distribute our "knowledge wealth" among all of our people, and in so doing achieve the true learning society, the "knowledge utility model" we have long advocated, where each learner has available—any time, anywhere, at the flip of a switch—the knowledge he or she needs for lifespan learning.

Much of what is needed to implement fully the potential of the learning society has been invented. The technology is available and generally in place. The next step requires leadership to establish cooperative, collaborative relationships and endeavors to build this lifespan learning network.

Our future requires inspired and creative leaders: men and women who are aware of the history, purpose, and social role of community colleges as "colleges of the people" and who are able to effectively utilize "cutting edge technologies" to build and sustain a true learning society.

References

American Association of Community and Junior Colleges, *Building Communities: A Vision for a New Century,* A Report of the Commission on the Future of Community Colleges (Washington, DC: AACJC), 1988.

Bennis, Warren, "A Personal Reflection: Peter Drucker" *New Management* 2(3) (Winter 1985): 21–26.

Bennis, Warren, "The Wallenda Factor" *Selections from New Management,* University of Southern California Graduate School of Business, 1985.

Bennis, Warren and Nanus, Burt, *Leaders* (New York, NY: Harper and Row), 1985.

Benezet, Louis T.; Katz, Joseph; and Magnusson, Frances W., *Style and Substance: Leadership and the College Presidency* (Washington, D.C.: American Council on Education), 1981.

Birnbaum, Robert, "The Reality and Illusion of Community College Leadership," In Eaton, Judith S., (ed.) *Colleges of Choice: The Enabling Impact of the Community College* (New York, NY: ACE/Macmillan), 1988.

Burns, James McGregor, *Leadership* (New York, NY: Harper and Row), 1978.

Campbell, J.P. (ed.), *Managerial Behavior, Performance and Effectiveness* (New York, NY: McGraw-Hill), 1970.

Cetron, M.J., *Schools of the Future: How American Business and Education Can Cooperate to Save our Schools* (New York, NY: McGraw Hill), 1984.

Diebold, John, *Making the Future Work* (New York: Simon and Schuster), 1984.

Duncan, Ann Huberty, "A Study to Identify Desired Leadership Competencies for Future Chief Executive Officers of American and Junior Colleges" doctoral dissertation, Pepperdine University, California, 1988.

Fiedler, Fred E., *A Theory of Leadership Effectiveness* (New York, NY: McGraw-Hill), 1967.

Flowers, Jr., Marshall E., "Perspectives in Leadership Effectiveness: An Application to Colleges and Universities," Unpublished paper, Claremont Graduate School, 1985.

Fryer, Jr., Thomas W., "An Overarching Purpose for Institutional Governance" *Leadership Abstracts* 1(11) (July 1988): 1–2.

Gardner, John W., "Leadership: A Collaborative Act" *New Management* 4(3) (Winter 1987): 11–17.

Gardner, John W., "Leadership: The Role of Community Colleges in Developing the Nation's Young Potential Leaders," reprinted from *Community, Technical, and Junior College Journal* 57(5) (April/May 1987).

Hershey, P. and Blanchard, K., *Management of Organizational Behavior: Utilizing Human Resources,* 4th ed. (Englewood Cliffs, NJ: Prentice-Hall), 1982.

Joseph, Earl, "Earl Joseph predicts: Training is a Growth Industry" *Training* 21 (10) (October 1984): 133–135.

Los Angeles Times, "On Defining Leadership," August 17, 1987.

Naisbitt, John, *Megatrends* (New York, NY: Warner Books), 1982.

Naisbitt, John and Aburdene, Patricia, *Reinventing the Corporation* (New York, NY: Warner Books), 1985.

Nielhouse, Oliver L., "Where Are All the Good Leaders?" *Management World* 16(2) (February/March 1987): 10–14.

Peters, Thomas J., *Leadership: Beyond Formulas* (Palo Alto, CA: Not Just Another Publishing Company), 1985.

Peters, Thomas J. and Waterman, Robert H., *In Search of Excellence* (New York, NY: Harper and Row), 1982.

Peters, Thomas J. and Austin, Nancy, "Excellence in School Leadership" *School Safety* (Spring 1987): 11–17.

Raymond, H. Allan, *Management in the Third Wave* (Glenview, IL: Scott, Foresman and Company), 1986.

Roueche, John E.; Baker III, George A.; and Rose, Robert R., "The Community College President as Transformational Leader: A National Study" *Community, Technical, and Junior College Journal* 58(5) (April/May 1988): 48–52.

Toffler, Alvin, *Previews and Promises* (New York, NY: Bantam Books), 1983.

Vaughan, George B., *The Community College Presidency* (New York, NY: ACE/Macmillan), 1986.

Walker, Donald E., *The Effective Administrator* (San Francisco, CA: Jossey-Bass), 1979.

Waterman, Jr., Robert., *The Renewal Factor: How the Best Get and Keep the Competitive Edge* (New York, NY: Bantam Books), 1987.

Ervin L. Harlacher is professor of higher education, Graduate School of Education and Psychology, Pepperdine University, Culver City, California.

PART II:
THE STATE
OF THE ART

6

A COMMUNICATIONS ARCHITECTURE FOR THE FUTURE: MARICOPA COMMUNITY COLLEGE DISTRICT

By Paul Elsner and Ron Bleed

There are several key trends in the world of communications technology: The first is *integration*. It is now essential that the communications technology networks integrate voice, video, and data. *Networking* is a key to success. Systems from a variety of vendors, and at different places, must be able to talk to each other in a digital form. *Access* to a wide world of information is becoming a requirement for the learner in the information age. Finally, *distinctions between departments* and functional groups within a collegiate organization *are blurring.* The technology of the information age is creating more one-stop services and multi-disciplinary instructional laboratories.

The Maricopa Community College District (MCCD) has developed several innovations in communications technology that position it well with regard to these major trends. The concept of a network was begun before networking became popular. The architecture to create smaller computer systems, centralized to the different colleges, was a first step four years ago. These systems were linked together with a network line that allows data to be transmitted transparently among the colleges. This particular architecture preceded the mass advent of the personal computer. However, when the personal computer came on the scene, this architecture was further extended with subnetworks of personal computers, decentralizing computing even further at each college.

This particular strategy was very effective because it matched the district's overall management philosophy. It was also on the leading edge of the development of that new type of technology. As the cost of computing came down, the concept of computing in smaller units became cost-effective. As this type of architecture continued to grow, decisions were made that encouraged standards. Fortunately, the standards became accepted and very popular in the communications industry.

Because of the success of the computing network, another network was established to support telecommunications. This involved the decentralization of telephone switches to the colleges. The same telecommunications network further enhanced the computing network by greatly accelerating the speed at which voice and video were transmitted among the colleges through a microwave system. Again, the telecommunications hardware selected was state-of-the-art equipment on the leading edge of the technology.

This basic networking architecture was also used to increase access to information by students and staff. Through the implementation of a network library automation project, information could be shared and accessed from any point. Information retrieval systems, computer conferencing, and external databases were extensions of this information access implementation.

This entire network concept has had significant impact on the organization. The network and all its associated hardware became a metaphor for change for many faculty and staff. The excitement of being on the leading edge led to a revitalization and renewal of many key personnel. There were many changes in attitude and a resurgence of enthusiasm. The new architecture represented a commitment by the organization to the future. This transformation of people will always be the most significant advantage of new technology.

A new era of management also came about through the improved communications. As a result of office automation, management became better informed about many issues. The geographic dispersion of the colleges and the tradition of autonomy would have led to increased isolation had it not been for the communications systems.

In the fall of 1985, MCCD was awarded a major partnership from Digital Equipment Corporation. This partnership consisted of large discounts on the purchase of both hardware and software. The purpose of the partnership was to create a model network for community colleges. MCCD was the only community college district among thirteen institutions of higher education selected to participate in this program. The agreement asked that MCCD provide deliverables, which are specific results that can be shared with other colleges. All the deliverables revolve around the effective use of computing technology, for instructional and administrative purposes, with the network as the backbone to all the projects. Information Associates joined the partnership and now provides software support for the development of deliverables. The following is a summary of the major projects.

Integration of All-In-1

All-In-1 is a software application that connects several standard office functions such as word processing, electronic message services, and desk management. All of these functions can be conveniently accessed from a central menu. This system has had a major impact upon the way colleges are managed. Personal communications have also improved.

Currently, over 600 employees use this software. Accounting summary information is accessible to district staff via the All-In-1 system. The Training Services Department conducts beginning, intermediate, and advanced sessions in credit and non-credit modes for new and continuing users. A Project Management System has been designed using All-In-1.

It is a goal of MCCD that over the next two years the use of All-In-1 will be extended to all full-time professional employees, including administrators and faculty throughout the district. In addition to its use as a work station, MCCD would like to extend the capabilities of All-In-1 to be used as a tool in the support of decision-making. The next steps are to define the additional types of information that will be displayed using this tool. Areas to be considered are enrollment, course, personnel, and planning information.

Budgeting Module

The goal of the budget module is to provide a tool to administrators that will assist them in the preparation and monitoring of the fiscal budget. At their work stations, they will be able to manipulate data through the use of spreadsheets, word processing, or graphics software. The system has been built and was used by staff in preparation of the budget for the current fiscal year. Continued enhancement and additional utilization of this module will be made.

Degree Audit System

There is a continuing need to provide advisement information to community college students. To address this need, MCCD has developed a Degree Audit System. The primary objective of the system is to assist students in course selection. In addition to its use as an advisement tool, the system is capable of performing graduation checks, statistical reporting, class load forecasting, articulation planning, and monitoring of the financial aid process. The data contained within this system are very useful in institutional planning and management.

Voice Registration

In an effort to continue the process of providing quality service to its student population, Maricopa has installed a system that enables the student to register for classes through the use of a telephone registration system. A Computer-Assisted Registration Line (CARL), which utilizes Touch Tone phones, has been implemented and used successfully at Rio Salado Community College and GateWay Community College. Students have been able to add and/or drop courses and request a summary of any actions other MCCD colleges take when they are ready to participate. Possible enhancements will be defined, such as bilingual registration, credit authorizations, address verification, alternate section selection for closed courses, and student account status.

Articulation System

The Articulate System project will develop an on-line electronic transcript transfer system through cooperative work with Arizona universities.

Student transcripts will be transmitted, and possibly evaluated, among these institutions. This project is currently under discussion. It is also possible that Maricopa will be the host for a statewide computer network of articulation agreements for all universities and community colleges. This is currently under study by a consulting firm from the MCCD Board of Regents.

Library Automation

Library Automation is a major system that provides for the automation of library and media center functions. The primary functions of this system will be to provide an online public access catalog, circulation control, acquisitions, and serials management. The software programs were purchased from DRA and the system has been implemented. The database has been converted to the new format.

The long-range goal will be to create a large information utility that will tie together MCCD libraries with others in the area, including the library at Arizona State University.

Telecommunications Improvement Project

To make these projects feasible requires the network to be fast and reliable. Telecommunication becomes a new highway over which information can be transmitted. MCCD entered into an agreement with U.S. West for a major improvement project for these highways. This will permit faculty or students to access the network at any number of places (offices, laboratories, or homes), and connect to a satellite computer to do a specific task. This flexibility and convenience of access opens the door to many new types of student services. Computer-assisted instruction, computer tools, and computer-managed learning are all part of the new instructional process. In addition, the service needs of the student can be met (registration, financial aid, and guidance counseling) through the network. Faculty have the same flexibility in accessing information. The resources of a library will be at the fingertips of the faculty, students, and community. The resources of neighboring institutions can also be accessed. MCCD currently has a strong network link to Arizona State University, and other universities will soon be added to that network. Instruction can be delivered to remote areas, regular classrooms, or various other meeting places.

Carnegie-Mellon University has also inaugurated a campuswide computing network that links students and faculty together. Their president, Richard M. Cyert, says that their network "will be seen as one of the most significant moves in education during this century." Their network is very similar to the one at MCCD. In both networks, students and faculty will be able to exchange electronic mail messages; call up bulletin board notices; receive and complete course assignments; write research papers; retrieve database information from files, libraries, and campus directories; and receive course instruction. Another similarity is that both networks are built upon one major vendor, but do support other vendors in a heterogeneous environment, using the equipment for many different purposes. The key to both networks also has been the rewiring of the colleges. MCCD and Carnegie-Mellon are each spending $6.5 million for the communication lines. At MCCD, these pathways consist of ethernet, fiber optics, microwave, and broadband cable.

At MCCD the project is organized by placing the major responsibility on the Information Technologies Executive Council, which has the responsibility for all computing, telecommunications, and library automation within the district. The members include a college president, three vice-chancellors, a faculty member, and a representative from Arizona State University. The Director of Information Technologies Services reports to the council. Staff responsible for those major areas report to the Director of Information Technologies Services.

Paul Elsner is chancellor, and Ron Bleed is director of information technologies, Maricopa Community College District, Phoenix, Arizona.

7

THERE IS A SATELLITE
IN YOUR FUTURE

.

By A. Robert DeHart

Business, government, and the media recognized the power of communicating by satellite in the 1970s, and today hundreds of satellites ring the planet in orbits 22,300 miles in space serving these enterprises. It is not surprising that large corporations and the federal government were the early users of this technology, simply because they were the only ones who could afford it. Mass manufacturing, however, has driven prices down in recent years and educational innovators are now discovering the enriching and effective power of satellite communication. Slade and Sanders (1986) foresee the developments before the next century of "a global college with thousands of campuses around the world exchanging and sharing interactively through satellites a dazzling array of international programming in every imaginable category." Lest you think this is a gross overstatement of technology zealots, stay tuned.

Telestar 301, Transponder 11, Frequency 4120 Vertical Polarity

Despite the complicated jargon, accessing a satellite is as simple as using a remote control on a home television set. How does it work? A viewer punches appropriate coordinates into a remote control switch and the receiver dish automatically seeks the right satellite and tunes in one of the thousands of programs being delivered daily by the necklace of satellites surrounding the earth. A dish can access any unscrambled program if it is tuned to the appropriate satellite. Commercial television, foreign broadcasts, teleconferences, sports events, congressional hearings, major cultural events, and a multitude of private and public programs are there for the taking. Most of these events are entertainment, and while many have educational value, not many are specifically designed for colleges and universities. But the number is growing.

For educators to originate programs for the college market, an "uplink" dish capable of transmitting a signal to a satellite is required. Uplinks are more expensive and there are far fewer of them than receive dishes, or "downlinks." While a good downlink can be purchased for $2,000 to $5,000, an uplink costs ten times that amount. In addition, a support studio is required for producing a program. Thus, there are two costs for originating a teleconference: the cost of the technology plus the cost associated with presenting a program. Colleges and universities are developing networks so they may share the expenses. But one should keep in mind when considering the uses of a receive dish that in addition to those programs specifically designed and marketed to colleges, there are hundreds of other good programs available for campus use. One only need peruse the satellite programming publications such as *Orbit* (which is nearer the size of a phone directory than the *TV Guide*) to discover the great potential for bringing the world to even the remotest campus.

While satellites provide accessibility on a scale not even imagined a few years ago, it is another feature, interaction, that makes this mode of delivery especially attractive to educators. When the combination of a satellite, television, and a telephone link are used together, people scattered over wide geographical areas can see and talk with one another at the same time. This event is called an interactive video teleconference. Such a teleconference originates in a television studio, a classroom, or a conference room where television cameras relay the program to an uplink dish which transmits to an orbiting satellite. A receive dish at a remote site picks up the signal and sends it by coaxial cable into an auditorium or classroom where the program can be seen on television monitors. There may be one receive site or hundreds, it makes no difference. Each receive site is also connected by telephone to the originating studio so that questions can be asked live and on the air. Teleconferencing is simply participatory television. Viewers can be actively involved by asking questions, clarifying, or debating. It is a way of bringing topics to people instead of people to topics as required in the face-to-face meeting for traditional conferences and workshops.

Easy communication among colleges without the need to travel, high quality staff development for faculty and administration, and the instructional delivery of telecourses to the remotest regions are destined to be the major educational uses of interactive teleconferencing. When these teleconference uses are coupled with the accessing of the great diversity of cultural, educational, and entertainment events available, the satellite can truly be seen as a major new learning resource of the '80s and '90s for both students and staff.

Dishing It Out

Current satellite programming is provided to colleges by three means: commercial networks specifically developed for the college market; college consortium networks developed for the college market; and commercial companies that assist any enterprise in offering a teleconference or other television event.

Unlike entertainment television or business teleconferences, programming designed for colleges is still in its infancy. However, experts tell us we're on the verge of an explosion in the use of satellite programming. Dean Robert Grey of the University of California, Los Angeles (UCLA) asserts that a major breakthrough using satellite delivery will bring an enormous variety both educational and entertaining, that "... we can only begin to imagine" (Slade, et al., 1986), and it is surprisingly easy for colleges to gain access to this programming once the maze of acronyms is mastered.

Commercial Networks Dedicated to College Programming

In 1985 the College Satellite Network (CSN) presented its first event, "The Congress: Is It Working?" to 100 campuses. Since then, several events have been aired. CSN's programming is free because it is underwritten by corporate sponsors. For more information call (312) 878-7300 or write CSN, 5547 North Ravenswood, Chicago, IL 60640-1199.

Campus Network (CN) uses a different approach by delivering its programs through two services: the National College Television (NCTV) and VideoCenter Events. NCTV sends, by satellite, a four-hour package each week to 170 campuses. The campuses videotape the package and rebroadcast it over their own campus network or over local cable television. The program is primarily entertainment and keyed to the younger college-age group. A place is left at frequent periods to allow colleges to insert local announcements and updates. Most colleges play the package several times during the week. CN claims NCTV programs currently reach two million students weekly and another four million people in cable homes.

VideoCenter Events, the second CN offering, operates much like a teleconference, though some events are not interactive. During the fall 1986 semester, such events as two feature films, a concert, a back-to-school video dance party, and an interactive debate on pornography were offered. CN plans to offer monthly events in the immediate future and eventually move to weekly programming.

CN's affiliates receive NCTV programming free since it is underwritten by corporate sponsors. VideoCenter Events charges vary from program to program and range from $100 to $500. A feature film costs $75. For more information on CN's programming, call (800) 223-1331, or write to Campus Network, 114 Fifth Avenue, New York, NY 10011.

College and University Consortia

There are hundreds of teleconferences offered every year for business, language, engineering, health, continuing education, and many other disciplines. These are often designed for a person practicing a profession in the discipline rather than for the teacher of a discipline, but almost every college department can benefit from these offerings if the information about them is collected and disseminated. There are several consortia developing around academic disciplines, but two major consortia are worth describing in some detail because of the quality and scope of their programming.

National University Teleconference Network (NUTN) is a nonprofit college and university consortium that, unlike CSN and CN, does not produce its own programs but shares programs by satellite that are produced by member institutions. The NUTN main office facilitates and publicizes teleconferences, but the member colleges put together the programs. The varied membership results in varied programming ranging across a whole host of topics.

On the average, NUTN member colleges pay $200 to $500 to receive a teleconference sponsored by the NUTN, though the range may be from $100 to $1,000, depending on the event. NUTN generally assumes that a college will pick up the cost for its staff, but just as happens in a non-satellite conference, students and outsiders will pay for viewing the teleconference. However, it is a local decision whether a college wishes to recover its cost through user fees. Occasionally a sponsor will underwrite costs for NUTN and the teleconference will be free.

A college does not have to belong to NUTN to receive teleconferences, but generally the teleconference fee is doubled for non-members. The full annual membership fee is $1,500 with a one-time initiation fee of $800. For this fee, NUTN provides such support services as training, marketing, programming aid, and technical advice. For more information, call (405) 624-5191 or write National University Teleconference Network, 330 Student Union, Oklahoma State University, Stillwater, OK 74078.

National Technological University (NTU) started about five years ago when twenty-four universities that included Georgia Tech, Michigan, the University of South Carolina, and Stanford, among others, began offering business and engineering courses to students and practicing engineers using their own uplinks. Students taking classes via satellite get the same syllabus, do the same homework, and take the same tests as those students who are in the classroom where the course originates. The big difference is that a student can receive a degree from NTU without leaving the receive site. More information can be obtained by contacting one of the participating universities.

Many other networks have emerged that have developed around special interests in college. *Orbit* lists regularly scheduled satellite programming for eighteen educational service channels. For example, there is a University Teleconference Network (UTN), a Health Service Network (HSN), and Public Broadcasting System's (PBS) The Learning Channel, which specializes in delivering telecourses. Most educators are familiar with telecourse programming over broadcast and cablecast channels since some 1,000 colleges and universities offer such courses. What many persons do not realize is that telecourses can be received by satellite as well. It is now possible for colleges that have not had the cooperation of local broadcasters and cablecasters to develop distant learning program centers by using satellite transmission directly.

Commercial Companies that Assist in Teleconferencing

Public Service Satellite Consortium (PSSC) is an example of a broker that doesn't produce teleconferences but offers training, technical support, technical publications, and assistance in planning. Membership dues are $500 per year and worth the money for those who want to start originating teleconferences and need advice, support, and marketing information.

Newly Developing Networks

Several consortia are forming to develop statewide networks. An example is California's 106 community colleges that are developing their own Community College Satellite Network (CCSN). Currently they have forty receive sites, with plans for a receive dish for every campus. The CCSN master plan calls for a fully functioning permanent state network to be in place by 1988-89 with the intention to connect with other state or regional community college networks in the future. For more information about CCSN, phone (408) 996-4426, or write CCSN, DeAnza College, 21250 Stevens Creek Blvd., Cupertino, CA 95014.

The American Association of Community and Junior Colleges is planning a national Community College Satellite Network, to be initiated in 1988-89. The network will operate as a formal coalition of community, technical, and junior colleges dedicated to the cooperative use of satellite technology. Among other activities, the network will encourage and assist member colleges in producing programs to be offered throughout the system; investigate group purchases of hardware and telecourses; publish satellite program information; and serve as a source of information on programs produced by and for community, technical, and junior colleges.

Clearly, a momentum is building for the creation of interrelated satellite networks that ultimately can link educational institutions throughout the country. The potential of such networking is both staggering and challenging.

The Instructional Telecommunication Consortium (ITC) is probably the single best source of information about all forms of television development in community colleges. It is an affiliate of the American Association of Community and Junior Colleges and can be reached by phone at (202) 293-7050 or by writing ITC, Suite 410, One Dupont Circle, N.W., Washington, D.C. 20036.

Institutionalizing the Use of the Satellite

For any innovation, someone in the organization must champion the introduction of that which is new. To organize and utilize satellite communication, a place in the college organization must be found that can plan, develop, implement, promote, and manage its great potential. At DeAnza College, the Learning Resource Center provides instructional support in many forms including print, audio-visual, computers, and television. Satellite programming is but one more learning resource in the arsenal currently managed by the Learning Resource Center. It seems appropriate for most colleges that this new medium take its place alongside the other media; however, the college is organized to manage them. One must admit that the push for developing satellite networks has not come from learning resource people; nevertheless, this would seem to be the proper permanent home. Almost everyone in a college will probably become a user of satellite television at some time, and that is a compelling reason for locating it in a general service facility rather than in some other unit, such as a television department. Technicians are not required to oversee satellite reception since the technology has been simplified to a point where the user can be a layman. The involvement of technology experts is necessary only if a college originates its own teleconferences.

Should a college purchase a satellite dish or explore other options such as leasing, renting, or borrowing? All of the above are possible, but purchasing is clearly the best long-term solution. Almost any size city has stores that sell and install satellite dishes at prices starting at about $2,000. There are two caveats. Make sure the installation site is properly checked out for possible microwave interference, and make sure to purchase a dish that will receive *both* the C-band and Ku-band satellites. Most commercial television is on C-band satellites, but Ku-band transmission is newer and will eventually result in lighter, cheaper, better, and more dual capacity, but well worth it.

While the dish you buy usually comes with enough cable to allow you to plug right into a monitor and start receiving, there are other things to consider in a permanent setup. A comfortable viewing room appropriate to the kind of program being received is important. People in groups do like large screens better than regular-sized monitors. If a concert is being viewed, good sound equipment is important. Lighting may be important for certain programming. An interactive program requires that a telephone be available and microphones may also be necessary. Finally, an experienced site coordinator needs to oversee the preparations and the conduct of special events and teleconferences. However, none of these requirements are particularly unusual for those who plan other kinds of college events.

While the emphasis of this article has been on *receiving* by colleges, *originating* will become commonplace as the cost of uplink transmitters continues to decline sharply. Colleges that have a curriculum in television production already have most of the equipment for producing teleconferences. Either permanent or portable uplink dishes (they are similar in appearance to the receive dish) need only be added to existing television studios for a college to become an organization site. The faculty and students in television classes will find it an easy transition to produce teleconferences. The cost of an uplink in 1988 was in the $200,000 range, but that price will continue to fall. An option for the time being is to borrow an uplink. In California there are several uplink transmitters in Silicon Valley business and government facilities near DeAnza College, and the college has produced several teleconferences on borrowed uplinks. In fact, the California Community College Satellite Network currently depends entirely on donated uplinks, or very inexpensive rental of uplinks, for all transmissions.

The 1990s

Colleges that recognize the opportunities for improving their educational programs and community services through this new medium will enjoy the challenge of shaping the future of educational satellite programming and reap the benefits that early adopters generally experience.

Though education is off to a slow start when compared to the sophisticated use of satellite communication by business, government, and the media, colleges will readily catch up simply because satellite communication is so effective and is becoming so inexpensive. The ability of college presidents in a large state to meet without arduous and costly travel, the ability of colleges to share faculty development workshops, the advantage of video library networking, the ability of faculty to see exemplary instructional programs located in the remotest colleges, the opening up of the world culture, entertainment, and education to rural colleges, the increased availability of telecourses at lower shared costs, and offering teleconferences to the people of our communities for all kinds of occupations and public interests—for all these compelling reasons and more, this technology will rapidly develop on college campuses. And the technology itself will continue to improve so that we can expect the screens to be larger and sharper, the telephone linkages more responsive and natural sounding, and sound systems to achieve all the qualities of actual presence.

There will be a satellite in every college's future.

References

Black, Randall, "Teleconferencing: Send Your Image, Not Yourself" *Science Digest* (March 1984): 5.

Cross, Thomas, "Teleconferencing Will Play A Key Role In Services From Intelligent Buildings" *Communication News* (February 1985): 78.

Satellite ORBIT, CommTele Publishing Company, P.O. Box 53, Boise, ID 83707.

Slade, Arthur, and Sanders, Kevin, "The Electric Campus" *Campus Activities Programming* 19 (3) (Fall, 1986).

A. Robert DeHart is president of DeAnza College, Cupertino, California.

8

FACILITATING THE INTEGRATION OF EMERGING TECHNOLOGIES WITH THE CURRICULUM AND INSTITUTION AT CUYAHOGA COMMUNITY COLLEGE

■

By Nolen M. Ellison and Marshall E. Drummond

Ohio's near disastrous industrial retrenchment between 1965 and 1980 has shaped the evolution of Cuyahoga Community College (CCC), as the college has responded to the loss of jobs and income to residents of central Ohio. Major policy decisions which now guide CCC's development are identified in the 1982–83 American Association of Community and Junior Colleges' (AACJC) Kellogg Foundation-funded national project, *Putting America Back to Work* (Parnell, et al. 1984). Linked with Ohio's strategic plans for economic development, CCC has made putting Cuyahoga County residents back to work its highest priority, through the creation of sound business/industry/college partnerships. At the same time, CCC is challenged to maintain high standards as well as open admissions in the pursuit of equity, access, and excellence.

The Process for Importing and Developing New Technologies into the Instructional Delivery System Environment

The physical center of all technology-related research and development activity at CCC is the Unified Technologies Center (UTC) at the college's Metro Campus. The UTC is an 85,000-square-foot facility managed as an auxiliary enterprise by CCC. The UTC is equipped with the latest in emerging technologies that support the manufacturing, medical, educational, and other related targeted market populations. A major role of UTC is to provide a process that will

- Monitor, access, and select emerging technologies that will become part of the UTC research and development mix;
- Establish the appropriate relationships and partnerships to aggregate the needed venture capital and support resources required for project success;
- Put the project into a matrix organization that will provide for project management and control, cost accounting, and profit planning, and will tie the project in with other ongoing research and development activities of the UTC;

- Provide the project team with the facilities and resources designated in the project proposal;

- Provide a means to distribute and market the resulting product to the CCC community and beyond.

The Assessment and Selection Process

The purpose of the assessment and selection process at UTC is to find projects that fit the scope of the enterprise, that appear to have a high probability of success, and that can be supported for the expected life of the project by one of the funding alternatives available to UTC. This process is presently maturing and ultimately will consist of three components:

- A "Technology Data Base," which will house as much information as possible about emerging technologies that bear on the markets and missions served by UTC. This data base will be a combination of locally stored and remote information (external data bases), which will be accessible through the college's existing computer network.

- A UTC senior staff steering committee, which will be composed of key managers from the college and UTC. This group will be charged with selecting projects and monitoring them as they progress from inception through final distribution.

- A senior level advisory group, which will provide the UTC steering committee with advice concerning the merit and likelihood of success of projects under consideration. This group will be composed of senior technical managers from specific industries that are targeted as UTC markets.

The assessment methodology used by the UTC senior staff steering committee will be a clone of the strategic planning process used by CCC for institution-wide projects (Eadie, et al., May 1982). The strategic planning process in use by CCC consists of several phases:

- *Scanning the environment*—the technology data base is reviewed for significant uses of new technology or for the redirecting of existing technology within the markets served. Suggestions for new directions come from UTC staff, members of the CCC faculty, advisory committee members, or other related persons.

- *Internal audit*—assess what is being done today in the specific field, determine what talent is available, what the interest level is, and what additional support facilities (people, places, things) would be required for the project.

- *Review specific markets and project proposals*—establish and set priorities.

- *Decision Point 1—determine the "goodness of fit"* of all proposals reviewed in the above process. Select proposals for further screening.

- *Formulate a proposal team* consisting of UTC and CCC faculty and/or staff, with advisory committee members as needed. This group is charged with formulating a tactical program plan.

- *Decision Point 2—the tactical program plan is assessed* for probable impact on resources and profit planning and a decision to proceed or cease investigation is reached.

The internal audit function is particularly important when dealing with new and emerging technologies because often there are no faculty or staff members who are up to speed with the technology. In these cases it may be necessary to form a partnership with outside developers who have a vested interest in disseminating the technology. In some cases the outside participants can partially transfer the knowledge base to UTC faculty or staff: in other cases the technology is so arcane that outside assistance will have to persist throughout the project development cycle.

Bringing all activities related to technological research and development into a single, coordinated structure is not without difficulty. Traditionally, faculty members have been encouraged to develop grants and manage projects in a very decentralized fashion. This sometimes aids creativity, but there are drawbacks to this decentralized approach, such as:

- *No ability to leverage resources.* Because many activities within different projects are basically the same, there is a distinct advantage to forming a research and development activity matrix that monitors resource requirements and intra-project leverage opportunities.

- *Project control is difficult.* Because each decentralized project is controlled by the person who received the grant, there is often little attention paid to accumulating detailed cost accounting or project information except that which is specifically required by the terms of the grant. This information is needed to attract venture capital for calculating payback periods and product pricing, and for profit planning, all of which are key elements for selling a project to a partnership of private investors.

- *Lack of senior management involvement* in make/buy and project redirection decisions. Grant-funded projects often have little leeway with regard to project redirection, but this is not the case with partnership-funded projects. The scale of the project can be expanded or reduced or the project can be terminated if experience shows that a questionable project was selected. Components of one project can be sold to another project if the specifications are basically the same. The ability to choose between making or buying a project component is made stronger by the fact that the technology data base catalogues project resources and makes the availability of resources quickly known.

Aggregating and Managing Venture Capital

UTC research and development projects can be funded by a variety of sources including: CCC operating funds; special state funds; federal funds; private venture funds, i.e. grants, foundations, societies, affiliated organizations; and partnership funds.

In addition to functioning as a technology-oriented grant development office, the UTC staff is able to provide custom services and products to a wide variety of customers. For instance, a firm may want to import a new technology and train workers for it. The UTC staff, working with the technical data base and advisory committee, would identify other organizations that might be interested in the same services, along with the vendors who will benefit from the potential transition. By marketing the concept of a joint venture to a number of potential participants, a business plan for a partnership can be created, complete with standard costs, estimated costs (new cost ingredients), payback period, and profit potential. If the resulting technology is one that fits the instructional mission of CCC, then the resulting product (i.e., consulting and training services), will be ultimately taken to the college curriculum by the faculty members of the team, and a predetermined amount will be charged for the intact instructional module. If the project is one that will not eventually be placed into the curriculum, the project must be self-funding with the caveat that profits from one project offset losses from another, if that is part of the overall strategic plan.

A project planning and control methodology can be used to uniformly monitor progress on all projects, and periodic project assessment reviews would be held by the UTC senior staff steering committee. A cost accounting system could be linked to project control and standard costs developed for purposes of product costs estimating, profit planning, and income statement generation. Costs can be refined as experience with the various cost components increases.

A Case Example—Development of the Computerized Librarian for Image and Media Electronic Transmission System

The Computerized Librarian for Image and Media Electronic Transmission (CLIMET) System is a step toward using properly designed wideband networks for the distribution of images and media stored on videodisc to a wide audience within the institution. The eventual outcome of the project will be the ability to use a computer network to distribute interactive videodisc data, images, and media throughout the network. This will enable a diverse audience to query and call up a vast variety of images, media, or data for projection on a large-screen, high resolution device or for reproduction by a laser or plotting device. For example, an art history professor could have the entire collection of the National Museum of Art at his or her fingertips, while an entomology professor would have a vast selection of high resolution images available to complement descriptions and examples. This system would have numerous advantages over conventional audio-visual techniques and distributed videodisc units, such as:

- Tremendous production cost savings over slides or other visual aid media (a large number of projects, such as the National Museum of Art, interactive videodisc project, are producing inexpensive videodiscs. For example, the entire art collection disc will cost approximately $300; equivalent slides cost over $5,000) (Optical Disks, February 1987).

- Cost savings and efficiencies in media preparation. There will be no manual cataloging or physical handling of the media. Media will be stored and accessed from a computer-controlled data base.

- Each user can create his or her own "slide shows" or presentations. Software developed in the CLIMET project will combine artificial intelligence with expert systems to guide the non-technical user through the process for maximum advantage.

- Existing facilities are being used. The required network configuration is already in place in many institutions. The only hardware requirements are disc storage units, disc controllers, network interfaces, a micro-computer, and projection or laser devices on the user end. In addition to this, the user hardware can be set up in a portable fashion, enabling further distribution of the medium.

The Selection Process

Interactive video projects are not new to CCC or to UTC. CCC faculty pioneered an interactive computer-controlled videotape biology program in the early 1980s (Burge and Wheeler, 1984). More recently, interactive video disc has been experimented with for a number of instructional applications, and several UTC partnerships have further developed the videodisc as an interactive training tool for technological applications. The strategic planning process applied to technologies related to videodisc applications is as follows:

- *Scanning the environment.* The technology data base was reviewed for significant use of videodisc or interactive videodisc technology. Specific attention was given to uses or potential uses of the technology that would permit the use of existing resources to the maximum extent possible. Suggestions for new directions came from

UTC staff, members of the CCC faculty, and advisory committee members.

- *Internal audit.* A review of videodisc-related projects underway or completed and an assessment of available technical talent in videodisc technology showed that a significant supply of expertise was on hand. In addition, due to the wide spread of mini-and microcomputers in the college network, there was increasing unused capacity on both the network and central data base facilities.

- *Information* from the processes described above was reviewed. Feasibility and time frames were established, and priorities were set.

- *A project team* was established that consisted of UTC and CCC faculty and advisory committee members. This group is charged with formulating a tactical program plan.

The UTC Senior Staff Steering Committee assessed the possibility of widespread distribution of high quality graphics, media, and images through the existing college computer network. This had a special appeal because the existing wideband network reached a great number of classroom and auditorium facilities, and the value of being able to deliver upon demand a rich and elegant selection of media was appealing. Tagged as a project for further examination by the Steering Committee, the feasibility and technological time-frame for such an undertaking was assessed by the UTC Advisory group and other UTC and college specialists in the technology. Additional input was sought from prime developers, and when all of this input was summarized and assessed it became apparent that the major hinderance to development was the lack of a computer controller that would permit the videodisc information to be accessed and processed by available computers with network architectures. Participants from Minnesota Mining and Manufacturing (3M) and Phillips Electronics disclosed the probable time frame for such capabilities at an IEEE Teleconference in February 1987 ("Optical Disks," February 1987). Still, without a specific project, venture capital could not be attracted, and the project awaited further technological developments.

On March 9, 1987, the Kodak Corporation announced a device that would permit videodisc access and media data transmission over a network controlled by Digital Equipment Corporation's VMS operating system. While this announced technology is not by any means the ultimate or final solution for computer-controlled network distribution of videodisc information, it is a beginning, and a meaningful prototype system could be configured using available emergent technology. The next step in the process was to establish the project team and attract the necessary venture capital.

The project is now at the venture capital attraction and funding phase. The prime developers (Kodak, DEC) are being invited to join with the college in the development and part ownership of the resulting product and process. In addition to this funding alternative, several grants are being pursued. While the project will be structured to operate without additional grant funds, the selection of the project for the grant funding would enlarge the scope of the alpha model.

Managing the import-export function for "cutting edge" technologies in the nation's community, technical, and junior colleges is one of the major challenges confronting senior administrators. As technologies in the workplace and the classroom become more important, the room for error in management and planning for technology diminishes. The impact of technology on the instructional process and the ultimate success of the college in fulfilling its mission has increased from a short list of affected curricula two decades ago to nearly every offering and service of the college today.

Among the difficult and significant challenges of managing technologies in the nation's community, technical, and junior colleges are

- Identifying and prioritizing relevant technologies;
- Finding the means (funding, staffing, technical support) to import selected technologies;
- Matching the technologies to the mission and plans of the institution;
- Adapting existing technologies whenever possible and effective;
- Finding ways and means to export specific technological applications or training to regional business, industry, and service organizations through partnerships or other contractual relationships;
- Managing and controlling the matrix of evolving technologies in a way that assures the optimal use of existing resources and eliminates duplication of effort whenever possible.

To meet these challenges, Cuyahoga Community College has chosen to use a centralized group of managers, marketers, instructional delivery teams, and technical support resources, which can be collectively managed for optimal use of resources and to provide accountability for service production and delivery. Further, the centralized focus permits the application of cohesive management structures and profit center accounting to the effort. If each piece of the technology import-export mechanism is evaluated on its delivery and profit making merits, then the overall UTC structure will reflect the success of its individual components.

References

Burge, M. and Wheeler, D., "Computer Controlled Interactive Videotape," Proceedings of the 4th Annual Conference on Applying New Technologies in Higher Education, Kansas State University, Manhattan, Kansas, 1984.

Official Plan of Cuyahoga Community College, "Third Decade Direction" Cuyahoga Community College Board of Trustees, October, 1984.

Eadie, D.; Ellison, N.; Brown, G., "Incremental Strategic Planning: A Creative Adaptation," *Planning Review,* (May, 1987).

Ellison, N.M. and Smith, J.D., "Implementing Strategic Planning—A Case Study for Institutional Change at Cuyahoga Community College" *Thresholds of Education* 9(4), (November, 1985): 19–24.

"Optical Discs: An Information Revolution," A teleconference and outline prepared by the Institute of Electronics Engineers, Inc. (IEEE) February, 1987.

Parnell, Dale, et al., *Putting America Book to Work—A Report and Guidebook,* (Washington, D.C.: AACJC), 1984.

Nolen M. Ellison is president of Cuyahoga Community College in Cleveland, Ohio, and Marshall E. Drummond is a professor at Eastern Washington University and principal consultant of Technology Specialists Incorporated in Pullman, Washington.

9

PIKES PEAK COMMUNITY COLLEGE: A CASE STUDY IN TECHNOLOGY INTEGRATION

.

By Cecil Groves

"Make no little plans; they have no magic to stir men's blood," states a planning prospectus for Pikes Peak Community College (PPCC). Since fall 1985, PPCC has been busy forming and implementing a vision of "what it can be" in meeting student needs. In meeting those needs, PPCC is employing the integrative and convergent capabilities of two cutting edge technologies—computers and telecommunications. College administrators believe the plans are bold enough to ". . . stir men's blood," but practical and utilitarian enough to be implemented.

The Setting

Pikes Peak Community College, in Colorado Springs, Colorado, enrolls 3,560 full-time equivalent (FTE) college credit students, with a student headcount of 6,580. Student enrollments in the 1987 spring semester were about evenly divided between occupational and transfer majors.

PPCC offers a wide array of traditional degrees in numerous disciplines and programs. The college has been identified as the High Tech Training Center for microelectronics in Colorado and hosts a consortium of twenty-one post-secondary educational institutions. PPCC provides resident instruction for more than 500 high school juniors and seniors in more than twenty-five occupational programs on a daily basis. Another special feature of PPCC is that since its inception, the college has provided educational services to military installations both in-state and out-of-state. A major feature of that service is the Student Work Experience Evaluation Program (SWEEP). The military programs and noncredit enrollments account for another 2,000 to 3,000 student enrollments each semester.

Colorado Springs, with a population of 325,000, has been identified as a megatrend city. Electronics manufacturing industries employ nearly 20 percent of the work force. The Consolidated Space Operations Center (CSOC) and the Northern American Defense Command (NORAD) also make their home here. These military operations and the associated research and manufacturing opportunities will continue to grow and to require a continually better-educated work force.

"No Little Plan": The Integration of Computers and Telecommunications

A review of literature, a survey of business and industry, and a routinized environmental scanning process identified needed curricular changes and found that future employment will require students to have a broader background of general educational skills (e.g. reading, communications, computation); a system orientation for the technical and vocational work force; literacy in the use of computers and telecommunications; and the ability to actively participate in decision making. A relevant educational program for the future must integrate all of the preceding actors into the curriculum.

Like most colleges and schools, PPCC had focused its efforts on increased program specialization. In the occupational area, specialization had manifested itself largely in equipment-specific programs with few knowledge skills that could be transported to other disciplines. With increased state funding to support increased program specialization through equipment acquisition, and with a changing workplace requiring a more flexible work force, the college was forced to rethink its curricula and instructional plans and strategies.

Computers and telecommunications were identified as the most important technologies (megatechnologies) which will impact both the workplace and the home. Student literacy in the use of these technologies was considered essential for long-term success and workplace flexibility. Because of the pervasiveness of computers and telecommunications (they apply to all industries and can be applied to existing equipment) and their integration (ability to link and coordinate separate functions), technological literacy, now considered essential for manufacturing employment, was also considered to be soon essential for service-sector employment. The use of computers and telecommunications by students was believed to be analogous to a student taking driver education: in order to be a safe and good driver, one does not have to be able to repair the car.

While computers and telecommunications were curricular considerations, their use was believed to be equally important in the delivery of instruction. Like many other institutions, PPCC had limited use of computer-based, computer-managed, and computer-aided instruction in different sectors of the college, as well as the typical programming courses and introduction to computer classes. These traditional applications of computers to instruction were primarily specialized or vertical and within a select discipline or program. Sharing and cross-fertilization of ideas and applications for computer use and application were minimal.

To maximize human and capital resources, better integration of computers and telecommunications and an organizational structure and culture supportive of both human and electronic networks was needed. This would necessitate both a hardware and software integration strategy, complemented by an entrepreneurial management strategy. An important outcome of such a learning and work environment was the potential for major breakthroughs in student learning.

To build a supportive administrative environment at PPCC, the president wrote a weekly article in the college newsletter which often focused on technological advances. For example, almost every day a new breakthrough occurs that has instructional applications. The question is, "Who will make those applications?" PPCC believes that it will not be the publishers, the universities, the hardware or software vendors, nor the federally funded demonstration sites. It will most likely be individuals on the local campuses who, in collaboration with their colleagues, will make those applications a reality. A mass of dollars spent on technological innovation will not spawn the instructional breakthroughs as much as a critical mass of faculty, administrators, and students who are able to network their ideas and applications with others.

Creating the Critical Mass

In 1985 PPCC began a systematic process, funded by a state grant, to educate and train more than sixty occupational faculty in the production of videotaped instructional programs. During this training, faculty also took courses in computer literacy. These activities correspond with the implementation of a totally integrated administrative and student services computing system—Series Z. PPCC was thrust almost overnight into the generally pervasive use of computers across the campus. Since 1985 the college has been individually and collectively going through a major learning curve progression and, at time, regression.

These changes have led to the internal identification of a number of persons who might be referred to as the hardware hackers, software hackers, MS-DOS hackers, and application hackers. Not one of these hackers work in the college computer center, nor do they emerge from the professional computer majors. Some are technical specialists or aides in electronics or the learning resources center, some are vocational or technical faculty who now find that they would rather tinker with a computer than a carburetor, some are misplaced academicians from the humanities or communications who simply like the order computers can bring to things, and there are those who have been playing with computers a long time but did not tell anyone until now. These are the folks who are forming the critical mass at PPCC. They cross the traditional instructional division boundaries and share a common willingness to try something new. Interestingly, this critical mass of folks is not easily described in terms of age, sex, or level of education. However, in general, the hardware hackers and software hackers have a stronger technical education background and are more comfortable with electronics.

Computers and Telecommunications: Efforts At Technology Integration

The following are not inclusive, but do represent examples of the general direction being taken by the college in integrating different aspects of technology in the classroom.

Video Based/Computer-Aided Automotive, Welding, and Machining Instruction: With video production skills provided through in-service training and with the acquisition of video equipment through a grant, faculty in the automotive area developed an engine building program. The program is videotaped and computer-based, permitting open-entry and open-exit to the course. All aspects of this program were developed and implemented by the automotive faculty.

Using some purchased materials in producing most of their own programs, the welding and machining staff have developed similar video tape and computer-based programs. Other occupational programs planning to use the technology as an instructional tool include carpentry and food management services. The occupational faculty who developed the preceding programs are now comfortable in authoring systems, integrating video with computer-aided instruction, and producing high quality video production.

Development Studies/Instructional Technology: This program received a $50,000 grant from the Colorado Commission of Higher Education. In addition, this program received Title III funds to assist the college in its overall use of instructional technology. Specific to this task, PPCC is working with the United States Air Force Academy in its development of the largest local area network (LANS) ever attempted by an educational institution. The academy will provide each cadet with a personal computer, high resolution color monitor, compact disc player, and direct networked access to faculty, other students, and academy resources. Instructional software being developed by the academy will be in the public domain and accessible. A primary feature of the academy software is its advanced use of graphics for instruction in such areas as calculus and physics. It is PPCC's goal to transport and modify where needed applicable software and hardware technology from the academy to the college.

Electronic Studio/Computer Graphics: The college has very strong programs in broadcast technology, journalism, commercial art, marketing, and graphics technology, all service components of the economy that are forecast to grow significantly and provide a substantial employment base. Each of the program areas has introduced the computer and, to some degree, computer-generated graphics into its curriculum. While each program will remain separate, the concept of an electronic studio as an integrating medium will permit the integration of different aspects of each discipline. The convergence of unique skills and knowledge from different program areas will broaden the perspective and application knowledge of students. For example, the electronic studio of the future will feature a combination of people, systems, facilities, and support for clients. Some of the people in the electronic studio will include art directors, authors, editors, graphic designers, computer artists, illustrators, draftsmen, animators, photographers, audio-visual specialists, and even computer programmers. Curricular considerations will focus on content services, production services, and distribution services, which will give students the greatest possible transference of knowledge and skills.

Microcomputer-Based Telecommunications Network: The college has developed several microcomputer-based telecommunications networks for internal local area networks and for national and international use and application. At the college, an Area Vocational Program network (AVPnet) is being developed to permit more advanced classroom management applications for faculty working with the more than 500 high school students who are bused to the college daily for occupational instruction. Public schools require extensive recordkeeping, which can interfere with needed instructional time and the teacher's energy. Each of the thirty-four teachers will be provided with a portable microcomputer, and a local area network (AVPnet) is being designed to operate by menu (one finger technology). Using bar code technology, for example, the teacher will need only to use a wand bar to find the student's name and information and make necessary one finger entries which will be downloaded to a "server" at the central office. Finally, the college has equipped an AVP school bus with telecommunications and computer hardware to permit student learning while the bus is in transit to and from the campus.

In other applications of computer and telecommunications technology, a local area network (LANS) has been created for students working in the business laboratory so that they might access work and lab assignments and communicate with the instructor directly through the network. The same concept, but on a much larger scale, is being developed for the journalism laboratory, where five to ten microcomputers will be networked with graphics production hardware. This laboratory will provide for full desktop publishing capabilities, newspaper standard pagination and production, broadcast-linked managed news production (PPCC has it own student-managed radio station, KEPC), and capacity to transmit video and digitally recorded images.

Local, statewide, and national menus have been developed for a high technology network called "TECnet," which will focus on curricula and program development. This network will include corporate membership by human resource development and training officers. Other networks and submenus being planned include those for international exchange between students (electronic pen pal program), developmental studies, and economic development activities and programs. All of the preceding networking activities will be greatly facilitated by the installation in 1987 of a digitally based telephone communication system for the college.

Pikes Peak Community College wants its students to be prepared, at whatever age, to successfully cope with the new information-based society.

Its goals are to use technology as an instructional tool rather than as an end-in-itself and to prepare students to comfortably use technology in the work force and in their everyday lives. Learning has become essential to assure the highest quality of life. To the degree that a student understands, appreciates, and enjoys learning, PPCC has provided that student with the necessary tools to ensure success.

Cecil Groves is president of Pikes Peak Community College, Colorado Springs, Colorado.

10

HIGH TECHNOLOGY: EVOLUTIONARY IMPACT ON TEACHING AND LEARNING

■

By J. Terence Kelly

High technology abounds at Miami-Dade Community College's North Campus, the first and one of four campuses in the Miami-Dade system. A microwave tower dominating the campus beams the college's video and digital data and telephone communications among all of the campuses. There are closed-circuit television channels that feature the daily activities of the campus. The library uses the newest technology in information retrieval. The campus has the latest in desktop publishing, computerized typesetting systems, and electronic and telephone mail. There are receiving dishes that capture a variety of satellite transmissions for student, faculty, and community use. A touch-tone, computerized telephone registration system is in place. Microcomputers, as well as several word-processing centers, are located throughout the campus. The campus operates a computer repair and maintenance program for its own equipment.

For the last decade, the college has been a recognized leader in the development and application of a mainframe computer-based management instructional system—Response System with Variable Prescriptions (RSVP) (Kelly and Anandam, 1976). From the mainframe RSVP system, a microcomputer-based instructional system with the capacity for individualization was developed at Miami-Dade. The system, known as CAMELOT, has unlimited capability for administrative and instructional applications.

Miami-Dade has always enjoyed a national reputation for specialized uses of technology for teaching and learning. The college was one of the pioneers in the development of instructional television, both in the production of high quality series and in the sophistication of delivery systems to support distant learners (Kelly and Anandam, 1979).

However, the fundamental nature of the enterprise has not changed appreciably. If one walked onto the campus and randomly opened classroom doors, one would very likely discover the majority of teaching and learning taking place in more or less the same modes that it has for years—the teacher in the front of the classroom with chalk and a blackboard.

The development of technology, the equipment proliferation, and the advancements that are made from day-to-day video, computers, and communication systems are revolutionary, and their implementation into the heart of the teaching and learning program is evolutionary (Kelly and Anandam, 1984).

High technology at Miami-Dade can be described as surrounding the campus environment but not fully penetrating the teaching and learning systems. A computerized Advisement and Graduation Information System (AGIS) has allowed the faculty to spend more time with students, leaving the computerized system to communicate the technical aspects of academic advisement. This AGIS system has been replicated in various degrees of sophistication in other colleges and universities around the country.

AGIS was one of the first comprehensive systems to outline course requirements and to audit graduation progress. The system lets students know what kinds and types of courses they have completed and are enrolled in, and which count and do not count toward degrees. The system serves as a superb advisement tool for students who desire to transfer within the state of Florida. Through this system, Miami-Dade strives to improve its graduation rate and is doing so with continued improvement and fine tuning of the AGIS system. (Schinoff and Kelly, 1982).

An early-warning computerized system, ALERT, is a mainframe database system that communicates with faculty and students. At midterm, every credit student receives an individualized letter that conveys the student's progress to date in each class and provides specific advice.

One of the most exciting projects at Miami-Dade North is a cooperative arrangement with the Educational Testing Services (ETS) to change their standardized national testing program to an interactive computer-based process for more individualized testing. This collaborative effort requires the sharing of facilities and personnel as well as a joint planning process to determine the practicality of ETS moving its mass testing program to a variety of adaptive-style testing capabilities.

Technology is becoming pervasive on the campus. There is virtually no academic or occupational area where one cannot see emerging implications that, in a relatively short time, are going to change dramatically the fundamental nature of the enterprise. For example, the chemistry department is faced with the tremendous task of moving into a new era of high technology support. Currently, the department is designing a new program on the use of modern chemical instruments of analysis for technicians and local industry research manufacturing operations. The courses in chemistry emphasize theory and wet methods of analysis as a service to pre-med and pre-engineering students. However, a large labor force of technicians working in numerous large and small industries is in need of more modern methods of chemical instrumentation. The impetus for this is described by the American Chemical Society's president, Dr. Mary Good:

> There has been a major evolution in the field of chemistry from the traditional use of test tubes, flasks, beakers, and balances, to sophisticated instrumental procedures, use of computers, and automation. This shift has changed the manpower and training needs of industry, and two-year colleges are well-positioned to meet the new needs of industry, research, and medical laboratories. (Good, 1986)

One of the monumental challenges facing the faculty and administration on the campus is the conversion to a high tech mode in more than 50 different occupational programs. Compounding the problem is the fact that many of the facilities that were constructed in the early 1960s are no longer functional. A local electronics corporation just a few years ago employed seventy-four engineering draftsmen. Today it employs three. The rest of the work is performed by eight individuals who use the computer exclusively for drafting work. It should also be noted that many of the traditional engineers today are not experts in data processing or typing but use existing software and application packages.

One of the more dramatic facilities-conversion needs is in the field of printing. Once there was a need for the open factory, "dirty" laboratory setting, which involved hand typesetting and a large paste-up area. The industry now uses a modern antiseptic laboratory to accommodate computer typesetting and graphic design equipment.

Expansion of computer graphics has had an impact on many disciplines. The faculty are developing teaching models for integrating the computer into radio and television, fashion design, business graphics, desktop publishing, and computer programming of graphic images. Calculational software and linear drawings in black-and-white were considered standard uses for computers less than two years ago. Now, all areas involve usage of three-dimensional animated imagery in as many colors as possible.

The occupational faculty are currently meeting the challenges of using high technology in a variety of creative ways. The Travel and Tourism Management Program currently is using the System One Direct Access computerized reservation system for its classroom instruction. This system is connected directly to Eastern Airlines and allows for the simulation of making air, hotel, car, and cruise reservations.

Faculty envision reliance in the near future on laser videodisc technology in a manner that has never before been offered to the travel industry. At a touch of a button a travel agent can instantly access a client's desired travel destination. Using motion and still photos plus text frames, one instantly can become familiar with travel destinations such as a view of geographical locations, various hotel accommodations, and transportation modes.

The aviation department's career pilot curriculum operates five full-motion simulators. Faculty recently developed an interface between the simulator and a microcomputer. This project, known as "Project One," involves the continuous monitoring of airspeed, altitude, and heading by the computer during flight. Additionally, a multi-voice synthesizer with multiple voice capability (male, female, high pitch, low pitch) has allowed simulation of an air traffic controller and the instructor. Future plans will result in different controller voices as the flight is handed off from tower to department and enroute controllers.

This innovative interface results in a pre-programmed flight plan which is given to the student by the "controller." The student is given specific airspeed, altitude, and heading for each leg of the flight. Once checklists are complete and the simulator is "airborne," the computer constantly monitors the student's performance.

While the North Campus today can be proud that it has been designated by the state of Florida as a Center of Excellence for electronics and high technology, the attention to the fundamentals of teaching should ensure that Miami-Dade North will continue to fulfill its mission. Reliance on high technology will enhance the most important aspect of teaching and learning—human interaction.

References

Anandam, Kamala and Kelly, J. Terence, "Communicating with Distant Learners," Yarrington, Roger (ed.) (Washington, D.C.: American Association of Community and Junior Colleges), February, 1979.

Good, Mary L., "The Next Twenty-five Years in Chemistry and Chemical Education," 2YC Distillate, A Newsletter for Two-Year College Chemistry Educators," American Chemical Society, 1986.

Kelly, J. Terence and Anandam, Kamala, "Response System with Variable Prescriptions (RSV): A Faculty-Computer Partnership for Enhancement of Individualized Instruction," Capoeric, 1976.

Kelly, J. Terence and Anandam, Kamala, "Taking Advantage of Emerging Educational Technologies," in *New Directions for Higher Education* (San Francisco: Jossey-Bass Publishers), 1984.

Luckenbill, Jeffrey D. and McCabe, Robert H., *General Education in a Changing Society* (Dubuque, I: Kendall/Hunt), 1978.

McCabe, Robert H., "Organizing Miami-Dade Community College to Emphasize Faculty/Student Performance," unpublished report, Miami-Dade Community College, Florida, 1987.

Schinoff, Richard and Kelly, J. Terence, "Improving Academic Advisement and Transfer Articulation Through Technology," in *New Directions for Community College Series*, X, (3), Sequence #39 (San Francisco: Jossey-Bass Publishers), 1982.

J. Terence Kelly is vice president and chief executive officer of Miami-Dade Community College, North Campus, Miami, Florida.

11

EDUCATION AND COMMUNICATIONS TECHNOLOGIES: A CHALLENGE

■

By William McIntosh

Books will soon be eliminated in the schools. Scholars will soon be instructed through the eye. It is possible to teach every branch of human knowledge with the motion picture. Our school system will be completely changed in ten years.

(Thomas Edison, 1913)

The philosophy of the North Carolina Community College System encompasses an open-door policy and the notion that learning is a lifelong process. An interpretation of this philosophy is that the North Carolina Community College System has a goal of providing educational opportunities for 6.5 million citizens for as long as they live. This, of course, is unrealistic in terms of simple economics, assuming that education continues to proceed in the future as it has in the past—with an instructor, a course, and twenty to thirty students.

In 1974 Central Piedmont Community College (CPCC) became involved in a search for economical alternatives to traditional educational practices by recognizing possible uses of communications technology. Since that time, CPCC has been involved in testing various technologies in terms of their technical, economic, and operational feasibility. The college has been actively involved in experiments using broadcast television, cablecasting, SCA FM broadcasting, cable radio, audio conferencing, video conferencing, ITFS, and satellite reception distribution.

In addition to the technological involvement, considerable resources have been expended in the acquisition and development of appropriate software. Software was obtained through licensing arrangements with software developers and distributors, work with various local and national consortia, and in-house productions.

Courseware and technology have been brought together in various teaching and learning strategies to determine the effects of various mixes of technology and traditional lectures. Strategies have also been extended from the previous use of technologies as the sole delivery mechanism to 100 percent lectures, with technology used as a supplementary or remedial adjunct.

Staff development programs were designed and implemented to assist faculty in the use of technology. These programs involved visits to various campuses in North Carolina and across the nation, workshops offered by equipment and software vendors, and in-house seminars.

Faculty who were involved received release time, reduced teaching loads, or extra compensation during the time covered by the experiments. A few faculty became involved without extra compensation and conducted the technological classes as part of a regular teaching load.

In retrospect there were a few surprises. The technology was available, it was reliable, it was effective, and it was economical when compared to the cost of a traditional education. There were no significant differences in learning exhibited by students involved in technologically delivered instruction and students involved in traditional classroom activities. Some students enjoyed the technological approach and wanted more of it; others preferred the traditional classroom; and for others it seemed to make little difference as long as the teacher was available to assist them with difficulties.

Faculty enthusiasm, motivation, and support on a continuing basis were directly proportional to the type and amount of incentives provided. Initially, the programs offered opportunities for travel, interaction with colleagues from other institutions, local and national recognition through writings in professional journals, and a feeling of being on the "cutting edge." As incentives were reduced and eventually eliminated, so was faculty involvement. And why not?

Teaching in a traditional classroom setting is, for many, an ideal job. The teacher controls the pace of delivery and, to a large extent, the quality and character of instructional materials. The teacher knows at all times the limits of exposure. The use of communications technology, on the other hand, transfers the pace of delivery to strict time constraints, requires media-adaptable course materials, demands a unique level of organization, and offers exposure to an uncontrolled environment (you never know who is watching).

The key to the successful use of communications technology is a highly motivated faculty. The current methods of compensating faculty for services rendered have served well for traditional instruction but are inadequate, ineffective, and unfair for practices that drastically change the teaching environment that most (if not all) faculty consider ideal.

It is likely that private enterprise, through the use of communications technology, will offer competing educational services to the general public. This is already happening to a limited extent and, when the profit formula is discovered, will expand in geometric proportions. When such an event occurs, the system of education will become consumer-driven, placing demands on the traditional institutions, and will be a motivator for change. Until such time, technology will be more productive in the instructional support areas than in the delivery of course content. To be wrong in this prediction is to keep company with Edison!

William McIntosh is vice president of planning, development, and evaluation at Central Piedmont Community College, Charlotte, North Carolina.

12

USING TECHNOLOGY TO SERVE RURAL AUDIENCES: THE JOHN WOOD COMMUNITY COLLEGE MODEL

By Paul R. Heath and Paul Kevin Heath

For many years, leaders in business, industry, and government have urged educators to modify their delivery systems to accommodate the needs of the adult distant learner. Constrained by sociological, geographical, economical, and workplace factors, adult distant learners have been discouraged from actively participating in higher education. Unfortunately, most educators teach as they have been taught, and, consequently, very little change in educational delivery systems has taken place in public or private education. Indeed, today a rectangular classroom with a teacher lecturing to thirty students is still the predominant form of learning in education.

Some change is beginning to take place, however, as educators adapt technology to the learning process, primarily because of the electronic revolution that has engulfed society. Today, 99 percent of all households in the United States have television sets and nearly 50 percent now have video cassette recorders, with personal computers readily available in homes, schools, libraries, and the workplace. The stage is being set for dramatic changes, and it would appear that if public educators do not seize the initiative, then new profit-motive proprietary agencies may emerge to capture the adult educational market, serving those individuals who are denied access because of time, space, and distance barriers.

Accepting the Challenge

In 1975, John Wood Community College (JWCC) accepted the challenge of providing services to the distant learner and has recently accelerated its programming through the use of telecommunications and computer-based individualized instructional programs.

The need for a nontraditional delivery system to serve the JWCC adult distant learner was obvious. The college, with its main campus in Quincy, Illinois, serves a district that lies between the Illinois River on the east and the Mississippi River on the west, a distance of well over fifty miles. The north-south boundary exceeds one hundred miles.

The city of Quincy (population: 43,000) serves as the commercial, medical, cultural, and educational center of west central Illinois. The surrounding region is characterized by many small towns scattered across 2,000 square miles of countryside. The wide expanse of the district is typical of hundreds of community colleges across the United States, who face the challenge of designing new delivery systems that can meet the needs of the part-time adult learner.

The Common Market Concept

JWCC's first major effort in meeting distant learner needs was the development of the common market concept. Simply stated, this strategy pooled the resources of existing educational agencies, permitting JWCC students to attend classes on the campuses of nearby private colleges and proprietary schools. Such an arrangement allowed flexibility for the student and avoided program duplication.

The vehicle used for the collaborative common market effort was an educational service agreement, a legal contract that bound public, private, and proprietary agencies together to more effectively deliver traditional educational programs to a population scattered over a wide geographical area and—as importantly—to offer a variety of educational choices to a heterogenous student population that differed dramatically in age, ability, and lifestyle.

From a community perspective as well as from a student viewpoint, the educational common market has been highly successful. The JWCC students have received a quality education; the area consortium colleges have benefited from increased enrollments; and the performance of JWCC graduates has satisfied local employers.

Nontraditional Initiatives

Having contractually farmed out a number of traditional programs to consortium common market colleges, JWCC was in an ideal position to develop a variety of nontraditional courses, programs, and support services. New agencies joined the list of educational vendors, including hospitals, who provided wellness programs, emergency medical service training, and a dietary management curriculum. Other nontraditional agencies that contracted to teach in the common market consortium included a private physical fitness center, the YMCA, a dance studio, the Quincy Park District, and several businesses that revised, upgraded, and made available their in-house training programs for JWCC programming.

The most notable of the business and industrial adaptations was the Harris Corporation's Broadcast Electronics Technology Program. This unique collaborative effort merged highly technical electronics courses, taught by Harris Corporation personnel, with JWCC general education classes, thus blending into one curriculum a state-of-the-art associate degree program. The merger transformed a major corporation from a recruiter of technicians to a producer of two-year graduates. In addition to saving recruitment dollars, the corporation was paid for providing educational services to train home-grown talent.

The new common market concept of using nontraditional resources led to the implementation of several creative community-based programs, such as swine and beef management, home renovation and repair, fire sciences for volunteers, a banking curricula and savings and loan programs, plus a myriad of public service workshops and seminars that represented cooperative efforts between JWCC and various community agencies.

Open Learning

By bringing courses and support services to the workplace and to outreach locations, JWCC learned a valuable lesson: people respond to programs offered close to home. An unpublished JWCC study clearly indicates that as distance increases, the likelihood that a resident will enroll decreases. As a result, the college's "Project Outreach" has expanded over the years, with courses being offered in over a hundred locations including storefronts, churches, libraries and community centers.

Offering classes close to home was not enough, however, as the demands of job and family prevented many adults from meeting the traditional academic calendar and class schedule. JWCC responded by creating an individualized open learning center. An open-entry and open-exit, self-paced, media-supported mastery learning model was designed to create flexible learning opportunities with teaching and learning time blocks established around the student's time parameters rather than a teacher's schedule. The emphasis on time segments convenient to the user not only created a more flexible educational program but underscored a basic JWCC philosophical belief that students differ primarily in their rates of learning, not in their ability to learn.

The impact of the open learning center was dramatic, as adults enthusiastically responded to personalized learning opportunities. Today, 30 percent of the JWCC credit headcount is enrolled in individualized instruction with over eighty classes being offered to nearly 1,500 students.

Technology for Rural Audiences

A three-year Department of Education Title III grant enabled JWCC to create credit-bearing computer-based courses for many rural sites, including the small rural area high schools, public libraries, and various business locations. The design of the system calls for computer terminals connected to a fileserver at each location, with course materials stored on the fileserver. The student would sign on to the system, retrieve the next lesson in the course, and complete the interactive session. Upon completion, the student's progress would be stored on the system and transmitted via modems and telephone lines at night to a central minicomputer on the JWCC campus, to connect to a central computer at the main campus.

The following day, the teacher or facilitator would sign on to the system, review the lesson, evaluate it, and give further assignments and directions for the next lesson—all by electronic mail.

In addition to offering an array of individualized, open-entry open-exit courses to the distant learner, JWCC has recently been designated as a send and receive site for the CONVOCOM. CONVOCOM, a consortium formed to "convoke and communicate," is a microwave public educational television system that electronically connects a consortium of private and public colleges and universities in a large geographical area of West Central Illinois. It is now possible to offer two-way interactive televised classes that serve distant learners in a region that includes Rock Island, Peoria, Springfield, Quincy, Macomb, Galesburg, and all points in between. Future plans call for several community colleges to collaborate on course offerings for the interactive phase of the programming, as well as to coordinate the public broadcast for home study applications. There has also been preliminary discussion with public school officials and correctional center leaders to determine the future role of educational television for rural public schools and the state's correctional system.

Broadcast instruction offered through CONVOCOM is now limited by air time, but the potential of satellite and microwave technology, coupled with the storage capacity offered through home video recorders, unleashes a powerful tool for the distant learner. The technology is available; the real challenge will be to retain the human element in the process, as the JWCC open learning center experience demonstrates that the distant learner still requires substantial personal attention as the student proceeds through the learning objectives.

High Technology for the Workplace

Throughout the United States the alarm has been sounded for business and industry to become more competitive through the use of high technology applied to the manufacturing process. Computer-aided design/computer-aided manufacturing (CAD/CAM) applications, robotics, and production automation systems are now being developed and implemented to reduce labor costs and insure quality control.

Inherent in the implementation of new manufacturing processes is the challenge of not only providing educational training programs for a changing work force, but also providing technology transfer programs that assist industry in commercializing new applications of technology.

Industries located in rural areas pose special problems for technology transfer and training. First and foremost is the fact that rural industries tend to be less sophisticated and frequently require more technical assistance than their counterparts in metropolitan areas. They may also not have the financial support to implement the needed technology.

JWCC is attempting to bridge the gap by nudging local industries toward automated manufacturing cells, computer-aided design, software development centers, and special computer applications. The college is assuming a leadership role in adopting new technology by serving in a consulting capacity and forming advisory groups to brainstorm issues.

Ultimately, JWCC must face the challenge of developing a technology center laboratory as well as hiring faculty who are in tune with the needs of the industry. In that regard, the college is proposing a rather radical departure from the traditional on-campus laboratory by introducing a CAD/CAM lab at the Quincy Business Incubator. The college also intends to collaborate with Western Illinois University to insure that the training programs and coursework articulate. The intermingling of community college and university faculty will insure a greater range and depth of service and training than either party could achieve separately.

Finally, JWCC intends to provide entrepreneurs with the latest technology to support their new business ventures by locating the CAD/CAM laboratory in the incubator. The equipment will be available to small business operations on a time-share basis, and the center will offer consultant services from the community college and the university. The system will also access the Illinois Resource Network, a computer information base that can identify key industrial problem solvers throughout the state of Illinois. The college intends to develop the technology laboratory in a real world setting, giving the students hands-on applications to company product lines instead of simulation models.

The creation of a special laboratory for high technology applications requires a sizeable investment in facilities and equipment. JWCC proposes to reduce the outlay by using the incubator as the training site and by convincing local business and industry that pooling resources will provide a flexible, adaptable training model that will, in the long run, give the employers a quality product at a reasonable cost.

Future Challenges

John Wood Community College firmly believes that instructional technology and telecommunications have the potential to open up a wealth of learning opportunities, provided that:

- New materials and coursework are developed in a consortial manner in order to capture the expertise of diverse faculty and to reduce cost;

- Public and private institutions share in technological advances and delivery systems;

- Changes in technologies do not restrict or constrain the adult learners, but instead create new avenues of learning for adults;

- Higher education institutions assist teachers in bridging the gap between the new technologies and the old teaching methodology. Educational leaders must give strong support to show that the new technologies can serve teachers and learners alike by opening up new opportunities for the distant learners.

The technology revolution that has overwhelmed society now makes it possible to create dynamic learning environments for all students—even distant learners who are bound by time and space. JWCC believes strongly that academia must welcome and support new initiatives in telecommunications, video applications, satellite transmissions, and computer based programs. The key element in program development should be the amount of specificity in course content. If the courses are designed in a mastery learning format, based upon performance objectives, then there should be no difference in on-campus and off-campus courses for the distant learner.

Paul R. Heath is president of Elgin Community College, Elgin, Illinois, and Paul Kevin Heath is a graduate student at Michigan State University, East Lansing, Michigan.

13

INTERACTIVE VIDEOTAPE:
PERSPECTIVE AND PROMISE

.

By Cara Garcia

Imagine a videotape that presents safety procedures in a shop area. That tape can be divided into segments, one per safety procedure. A computer can state the procedure on the monitor and then show the procedure in action on the TV. After the video segment, the computer can test the student on the procedure and move on to the next one, repeat the same one, or reteach the same one with another example. The student's answers are scored and the student is told if he or she passes or needs more drill and practice with the procedures. This is learning with interactive videotape, a new instructional technology that allows students to tailor the learning experience to their own needs and interests. The preceding example is a very low level of learning (rote), which is nevertheless necessary for such needs as safety instruction or learning the campus, requirements for graduation, scholarships, and other important factual information. This type of instructional design comes from behavioral psychology, which treats learning as rote habit formation through drill and practice.

Recently, however, advances in instructional theory have taught us about instructional designs based on principles of cognitive psychology, which treat learning as a process leading to personal insight. An example of a cognitive approach would be a videotape that presents a story with alternative endings. The student selects the ending he or she thinks would be most preferable for the story. This lesson would encourage the student to think critically in order to select an ending. The insight gained from the program might be that the student realizes that stories are constructed by the author's choice, perhaps from several very good alternatives. When the student writes a story of his or her own, he or she will realize that there's more than one good ending and that writing is a process of decision making among alternatives.

It is not necessary to test students over what they have viewed. The same multiple-choice question format that is used to test the student could be used as a menu to ask the student to select the next segment of tape to be viewed. This increases student control over the viewing of the tape. From the cognitive perspective, the student must set his or her own purposes for viewing the tape; the tape is a means to an end, not an end in itself. The technology, as well as the information it conveys, is used as a tool to serve the student's purpose.

With interactive videotape, the viewer is active rather than passive during the viewing, the viewing is individualized, and a record of the session can be kept for the teacher to review later. The use of interactive videotape answers the nagging questions of: "What are the students gleaning from the video experience," and "Is this tape at the right level for the expertise and interest of the students?"

The Pepperdine Project

Recently, Pepperdine University has formed an Interactive Videotape Special Interest Group (IV-SIG). The members of the IV-SIG are either educators or corporate trainers. Based on the group's experiences and observations, there are basically three conditions in which a teacher could use interactive videotape: by making an existing tape interactive; by taping a guest speaker or student presentations and making the tape interactive; and by shooting a tape and making it interactive.

Making an Existing Tape Interactive

The current boom in commercial videotapes and programmable videotape recorders gives teachers many resources to draw on for instruction. But the student's attention must be focused on exactly how the video relates to the topic of the class. In the past, instructional media experts have suggested that the tape be showed in segments, stopping to point out how the upcoming segment would illustrate a point that students should learn, and that the tape be shown a second time without stopping. Now, by interfacing the videotape recorder to a microcomputer, the tape can be shown in segments as the experts have recommended, and it can also collect the comments, preferences, and reactions of the students who watch it.

Taping a Guest Speaker or Student Presentation and Making the Tape Interactive

This is a variation on the first theme. Imagine that you have had a guest speaker in your class. You've taped the session to not only help the absentees, but also because you don't want to impose on your guest every term. Now you can sit down with the computer authoring software, divide the guest's presentation into segments which are at least two minutes long, and create a few screens to intersperse between the segments of the guest's presentation. If the guest's speech was really twenty minutes long and then he spent the rest of the time answering questions, the twenty minutes might divide into five or six segments, one for each main idea the speaker presented. It would take about an hour's time to mark the tape, create information-presenting screens that tell the student what to watch for in each segment, and create a multiple-choice question after each segment.

Now you have a tape that can be used by absentees and future students alike. If you wish, you could assign the viewing of the tape as homework, using the technology to save classtime.

Shooting a Tape and Making it Interactive

For teachers who wish to create a tape which branches, a good knowledge of flow charting is helpful. Branches which show wrong responses as well as the right can be created. For example, imagine shooting a tape to teach CPR. Multiple-choice questions ask what the next step in the CPR process should be. If the student selects the wrong answer, the program shows a video segment of the dire consequences!

In working with the interactive videotape, the IV-SIG has thus far formulated some tentative findings. For the first two conditions above, there has been a three-to-one ratio of time to length of tape. It takes an hour to make a twenty-minute tape interactive. The other condition—shooting a tape and making it interactive, has a much greater ratio. Based on a one-time experience, it has taken three hours to flow chart the lesson, three hours to script it into a twenty-minute lesson, four hours to tape it, and four hours to make it interactive. At a ratio of 42:1, this condition should be regarded as a major undertaking by a teacher. However, because computer bugs plague software designers, and because it's easy to underestimate the time it will take to make a tape interactive, allow twice as much time as suggested in order to keep your hassle-factor low.

Is the interactive videotape worth the effort? The IV-SIG concludes at this point in time that teachers who use it can enhance the video experiences of their students. Videotape will be the economically feasible way to customize video presentations until other technology emerges. However, shooting a tape to make it interactive does not seem to be a practical undertaking by one teacher; such a project requires a team approach.

Cara Garcia is associate professor of higher education, Graduate School of Education and Psychology, Pepperdine University, Culver City, California.

PART III:
FUTURE LEADERSHIP
REQUIREMENTS

14

THE LEADER'S ROLE IN WELCOMING NEW TECHNOLOGY

.

By R. Jan LeCroy

The welcoming process is a familiar one to our culture. From time to time, virtually all of us welcome others into our homes, organizations, clubs, or churches. Since the dynamics of welcoming first involve inviting, we choose those we welcome to our groups. If the invitation is accepted, we begin to pay attention to that person. We create comfort for, spend time with, and designate a place—a physical space—for that person. At least during the initial get-acquainted process, we tend to act as a buffer, screening away unpleasantness whenever possible.

The leader who welcomes cutting edge technologies needs to perform many of the same functions within a learning community. The successful integration of a new technology into the organization will depend in good measure on how well the welcoming process is attended to.

The Dallas County Community College District (DCCCD) has a reputation for integrating and welcoming new technology into the overall life of the institution in an effective manner. Early on DCCCD pioneered the development of telecourses. Later it developed and routinized a sophisticated array of mainframe applications, and later still it put in place an institutionwide office automation system. More recently, the DCCCD has been involved in the development of touch-tone registration systems, new uses of educational software, low-powered TV, interactive video disc, ITFS (Instructional Television-Fixed Service) and, undergirding these recent developments, a highly sophisticated communications network. This network is perhaps the most dramatic example to date of the ways in which cutting edge technologies are integrated into the life of the institution.

The Leader's Core Responsibility

A leader who welcomes new technologies to his or her institution should observe the following.

- One must have clearly in mind a philosophic base that will help to make a decision. Basically, the decision is based on a vision, and students are at the center of that vision. Ask yourself and those working with you if the new technology will increase your ability to serve students with quality and productivity.

- Educate yourself about the technology. One needs to become not a specialist but a well-informed generalist who can then apply experience and expertise as an educator to the new technology.

- For more specialized input, rely on a core staff group who not only know the technology in more sophisticated ways, but who know you, your philosophic commitment, and the organization.

- Make the initial go or no-go decision virtually alone.

- Share the decision with as many professionals in your community as seems feasible and ask them to help devise the best process for testing and welcoming the new technology. When instructional applications are obvious, that must mean involving large numbers of faculty.

- During the implementation process, ask the institution to take small, incremental steps.

- Make sure there is as much expertise and consultative help as is needed to facilitate healthy implementation and to avoid depleting the organization's energy.

- Take personal responsibility for keeping the process from stalling. Even if certain steps are awkwardly accomplished, once commitment is made insist that the organization either move forward or admit that this particular project has failed. It is important to be able to admit failure from time to time.

Good Processes For Implementing Are Crucial

Since so much of this welcoming is predicated on good process skills, and since the leader sets the tone for the process of welcoming, here are eight more practical rules for welcoming with integrity and less wear and tear.

- *Prod* the organization gently to begin with. It is never easy to get started. Organizations, especially large ones, resist change and need to be nudged. That is a critical responsibility of its leadership.

- *Pilot* whenever possible. Such testing allows the organization to have a "shake down cruise" before large numbers are involved and a great deal of money is expended.

- *Piggyback* innovations. Any major technology in the DCCCD must be interactive with existing systems precisely so that piggybacking will be possible. What we have learned in telecourse development translates now to interactive software development since many of the same systems and personnel are involved. Overall, consciously ride the shoulders of innovations that have gone before.

- *Pull* applications together. Long ago the DCCCD determined that artificial delineations between use of administrative and educational technologies were counterproductive. The systems are designed to provide support across these artificial barriers. For example, the new communications network supports such varied applications as electronic mail and interactive classroom instruction.

- *Partner* as much as possible. DCCCD has learned to share the costs and demands of innovation with other colleges and universities. It has formed partnerships in the development of telecourses, educational software, and library automation.

- *Pioneer* when the vision is strongest. Currently DCCCD is developing computer-based tutoring systems—pioneering GED applications for community colleges because practice work in basic skills development is so critical an element in serving new student populations well.

- Look for *profit.* If the product and systems developed in-house are good enough, they can be shared and can generate revenue, making it possible to plow dollars back into development of similar or related technologies.

- *Pace* implementation in small, incremental steps. Staff participation and involvement are key from the very beginning. Any product development process needs to pull together likely users and involve them in implementation. Frequently, those involved become change agents and speed development by introducing the new technology to others.

A Model to Describe The Whole

In Richard Foster's book, *Innovation,* (Foster, 1986, pp. 101–102), he delineates the S-curve of an innovation. The S-curve is a descriptive model designed to pinpoint the limits of current technologies in order to better assess when to innovate, i.e. when to introduce new, cutting edge technologies. According to Foster, first efforts to launch an innovation, although necessary, generate little real change, are sometimes nonproductive or even counterproductive, and represent the base of the curve. Then, by taking incremental steps, the organization moves to the midpoint of the curve and efforts to innovate become more effective, efficient, and productive. After a time the innovation reaches a point near the top of the curve when its refinement produces less return or improvement, even though more organizational energy is expended in the refining process. It is at that point, or perhaps slightly before, that the organization needs to begin another S-curve, still relying on existing technologies but moving on to the next major innovation and its curve.

When DCCCD begins its own S-curve, it is generally in the business of piloting, piggybacking, and partnering. As the innovation develops, the organization looks for profit and paces the implementation process carefully and incrementally. As the organization nears the end of the S-curve, the push must come from the leader to begin again with another innovation, pioneering when it seems important to do so.

The Communications Network: A Case Study

The new state-of-the-art communications network is a system relying on intercampus (nine locations) microwave or fiberoptic transmission paths. Each location has digital switching equipment, which makes it possible to integrate voice and data transmissions through high technology. This enables one-way video and two-way audio application among various locations. The network elements include a low-powered TV station for transmission of instructional television courses for students in the country, and an Instructional Television Fixed Services (ITFS) station to transmit specialized industry training modules directly into local business and industry. Since all the communications equipment functions in the digital mode, the system has a great deal of flexibility. The microwave system carries all communications for voice, data, data processing, video, and includes all office automation functions as well.

The way in which DCCCD implemented its communications network illustrates more specifically how process skills have moved it along its own S-curve. This DCCCD communications network was first piloted at two locations for six months. The innovation, through its compatibility with existing DCCCD computer systems and hardware, piggybacked on earlier innovations. One application is being developed in partnership with WICAT and will eventually be shared with other colleges nationally. Products developed during the partnership will be state-of-the-art and highly marketable, thus opening the door for profit. In addition, over the eight-year period, the network will save $2 million on telephone bills. When one element of the network saves this kind of money, other dimensions can be seen as a bonus. Obviously, the network pulls together educational and administrative applications. For example, voice transmission will be possible in both the classrooms and the offices in the future.

The Leader as Catalyst

The chief executive of DCCCD plays a pivotal role in welcoming the technology. The role includes inviting, paying attention to, creating comfort, providing resources, and acting as a buffer. Such processes are critical. Surely the work is stimulating, but it is never easy. In fact, it would be wrong to suggest that the leader's role in welcoming new technology is an easy one.

Rather, the leader's role is to be a catalyst, to push the organization to risk—at least some of the time—to pay attention to the S-curve, and, when the time is right, to welcome new technologies. Certainly, it would be foolish not to listen to dissent, but the role is to keep moving so that the wait is not too long nor the risk too little. As a leader, it is one's responsibility to make clear that the ability to innovate is a requisite for growth; there can be no turning back when the use of new technology expands the likelihood that learning will flourish.

Reference

Foster, Richard, *Innovation: The Attacker's Advantage* (New York: Summit Books), 1986.

R. Jan LeCroy is president of the Dallas Citizens Council and former chancellor of the Dallas County Community College District, Dallas, Texas.

15

FUTURE ROLES OF
EXECUTIVE LEADERS

.

By Ervin L. Harlacher

The executive leader of the twenty-first century will be less a commander than a coach who "converts people and persuades them to shared values," according to Michael Silva and Craig Hickman, authors of *The Future 500 (Leadership Abstracts*, 1988).

Community college chief executives of tomorrow will play many roles in revitalizing their institutions and renewing the people within them. They will find themselves tuning into the environment to determine the future direction of the institution five or ten years down the road; articulating a creative vision for the organization that can serve as a "compass, a road map, a star" that gives purpose and direction to institutional efforts; developing a mission that focuses on students and their needs; translating that vision and mission into goals for the institution and expectations for students, faculty, and administrators; shaping the organizational culture and climate on the basis of individual values, institutional goals, and expectations; building coalitions, working with teams, and managing the conflicting demands of various constituencies by creatively integrating the legitimate needs and concerns of each group; and continuously monitoring progress and intervening in a supportive manner when necessary.

Coalition Governance

Colleges and universities today are viewed widely not as organizations, but as pluralistic democracies—political systems composed of various special interest groups and subgroups with differing goals and values.

The majority of literature in postsecondary education governance theory since the 1960s has limited its discussion to the bureaucratic and collegial (democratic or humanistic) models. While the bureaucratic model sees the college as a large, complex hierarchal organization, exhibiting at the top a clearly defined authority structure (board and president) that controls and directs the work of those below, the collegial model emphasizes a community of scholars, where decisions are made only after full deliberation by those affected by outcomes. The role of the president in the bureaucratic model is an autocratic leader whose image serves to reinforce organizational norms, rules, and ranks. In the collegial model, the leader is first among equals; his or her role is not to make decisions, but rather to move the group toward its ultimate goal, that of consensus (Birnbaum, 1988).

The work of Baldridge and others (1978) has suggested the need for a third governance model, given the defused and ambiguous nature of postsecondary education. The practice of colleges and universities, according to Baldridge, is to employ a large number of professionals who are closely identified with a discipline rather than with the institution and who are given to acting autonomously. While Cohen and March (1974) characterized this model as "organized anarchy," Baldridge provided a more useful scenario, describing the model as "political" in nature. The political model derives much of its empirical support from the open systems approach of the situation/contingency paradigm.

Political leaders "view their institutions as fragile coalitions that must constantly be tended and nurtured." They do this by fostering mutual respect among all the interest groups involved. They will not pit one group against another even to bolster their personal power. They don't take the support of any group for granted. They find out by talking to the various groups what decisions need to be made, and in the process build support for the outcomes. They know the difference between "political posturing" and legitimate claims. They recognize that there is "a time to act" and "a time to bravely sit still."

The role of the political leader is often conflict resolution—to help manage the process of compromise, collaboration, and mediation that leads to acceptance of the leader's own goals. The influence of the leader is limited by the political pressures of these groups, and the leader must spend time building positions that are supported by coalitions that change over time from issue to issue. The challenge of the executive leader in the political model is to avoid becoming isolated from his or her constituencies and to remain sensitive to the competing interests of a wide variety of special interest groups. When executive leaders become too distant and act independently from their internal or external constituencies, they discount the process for leadership effectiveness.

Under coalition governance, decision making and accountability are shared on many levels to achieve an "ownership" of decisions among diverse constituencies. Coalition governance is a means, not an end. The governance process is characterized by open communication and participative decision making. ". . . The missions of at least some institutions," according to Fryer (1988), ". . . prominently including community colleges—can usefully be accomplished through governance processes that involve more than structures and processes for control and direction."

Accordingly, coalition governance skills will be mandatory for future community college executive leaders. They will need to be able to lead the way through the organizational network and politics, to lead in many different directions simultaneously, and to lead different constituencies at the same time.

John W. Gardner has suggested that successful executive leaders have no choice but to exercise leadership across boundaries. "Ours is the world of multiple, colliding systems, and leadership beyond the leader's juris-diction is absolutely essential" (Desruisseaux, 1987, p. 30).

Future coalition leaders will need to maintain and nurture internal and external constituent networks and be able to successfully prepare and "sell" institutional proposals to internal and external political leaders. This requires communication and interaction with appropriate internal and external constituencies to ensure that pertinent information is shared at all levels. The internal population includes individuals and groups that have a stake in the everyday operation of the institution, e.g., students, faculty, board members, and administrators. The external constituencies include individuals, groups, organizations, and institutions in the community. The successful coalition leader is able to respond in a "catalytic" manner to the competing interests of labor and management, diminishing resources, and conflicting communities of interest by:

- Facilitating the emergence of a jointly supported set of objectives;
- Fostering group solidarity and commitment;
- Inspiring vision that can become the core of an insightful, commit-ment-generating strategic plan (Whetten, 1984, p. 40–42).

Effective coalition governance requires executive leaders to share leadership and play the role of politician.

Shared leadership. Shared leadership is interactive and interdependent. Future executive leaders, according to Bennis (1976), will see the need for collective leadership and will use a multiple-option approach to decision making; complex problems will be resolved through the use of executive constellations or task forces, which forge a new sense of esprit de corps. Kanter (1977) added that when teamwork and task force manage-ment are encouraged, the sharing of power is experienced by more and more people in the organization.

According to John W. Gardner (Desruisseaux, 1987), ". . . almost all of the talk about leadership suggests a solo performance, as if the leader is up there all alone. But if you observe institutions being led, you see a team. And beyond that team—in many healthy, well-functioning systems—there are further circles of people who are, in effect, sharing the leadership task, who are doing part of what it takes to make that system function" (p. 30).

Thomas Neff, president of Spencer Stuart, a New York executive-recruiting firm, has suggested that growing complexity "means no more room for the one-man-band CEO" (*Leadership Abstracts*, 1988).

The successful executive leader of the future will develop and partic-ipate in networks with other public, private, and community organiza-tions. Interagency cooperation will be both a theme and a resource. There is already a call in postsecondary education for intergovernmental col-laborative planning and actions to meet new societal needs—partnership arrangements among postsecondary education, community-based organi-zations, business and industry, labor representatives, and high schools.

Politicians. The future community college executive leader must also be a "miracle worker" in the political realm. "The bigger the corporation and the more global its sweep, the more its chief executive must be the consummate politician" (*Leadership Abstracts*, 1988). Arthur D. Little consultants have predicted that "the future belongs to the 'megacorporation' whose senior managers will concern themselves clearly with balancing the conglomerate's economic interests with those of the local culture."

In any public institution in which governance is shared between a hired professional and an elected or appointed board, the making of policy requires some level of political activity. Hammering out a consensus—and the tugging and pushing that accompanies this process—are political activities.

To enhance public confidence, educational leaders try to establish networks of groups and individuals who will support the mission of the institution and minimize any damage done by critics. Because of the occupational taboos, they define such activities as "public relations" when the accurate term is politics.

These executive leaders are politicians; they lead successfully by evaluating and influencing internal and external socioeconomic communities. They are political lobbyists. They tolerate environments filled with ambiguity, uncertainty, and complexity, which often place them in an uncomfortable role. If executive leaders think they are hip deep in a bog of complexity now, they are bound to flounder even further in the future. Cleveland (1972) predicted that future public executives will have to pick their way through the jungle of complexity and make policy as they go.

Whetton and Cameron (1985) observed that successful executive leaders are politically astute, pragmatic, and skillful negotiators, sensitive to the political shifts within the organization and the environment, flexible in their ideological orientation, and not adverse to "horse trading" with interest groups.

Fisher (1984) has pointed out a year earlier that while little emphasis had been placed on the "political" ability of college presidents, effective presidents were able to identify, cultivate, and be sensitive to the diverse needs of their public constituencies. Fisher concluded that understanding the needs of the external decision makers is crucial to the tenure of the educational leader: "no aspect of a presidency is more important than activities with external constituencies" (pp. 122–123).

Direction-Setting

Change-saturated environments exact a price! Both the intensity of change and the increasing diversity in the sources of change are dramatically affecting executive leaders, the institutions they lead, and the individuals within them. According to Joseph (1984), when we speed up the production of new knowledge, which is doubling every five years, we also speed up the production of change. The practical effect is the collapse of the lead time for planning while planning is in progress.

Predictions as actions, according to Martel (1986), should be based on a clear understanding of the change process, not the present, since the present will be different tomorrow. Adaptions seldom come easily, even when individuals and their organizations are receptive to change. People fear and resist any change that disrupts the status quo; they must be given an opportunity to work through the psychological implications of any change process in a gradual way over several months, and in so doing see what the change means personally for their present and future (Connor 1987). If they "... are to be led along a new path, it is essential that they understand and appreciate the need for change so that they can willingly relinquish their ties to the past" (Roueche, Baker, and Rose 1988, p. 51).

Executive leaders of tomorrow's community colleges will, therefore, need to know how to adapt to change within a complex, dynamic society and develop effective coping strategies to deal with change. Coping effectively with the turbulent times ahead, according to Toffler (1985), will require "radical leaders" who recognize the importance of discontinuity; who view tasks holistically; who see problems in relationship to each other and other variables; who are open to "unthinkable" solutions; and who are skillful at strategic planning and have the ability to cope with accelerated change.

Future executive leaders will need to make change a way of life—they will need to be "change masters" who not only adapt to change and inspire creative, innovative contributions, but also encourage others to use their initiative. The primary architect of change, according to Roueche, Baker, and Rose (1988), must be the president.

Direction-setting is the critical determinant of the organization's unity and effectiveness. Successful organizations set direction, not strategy. Getting everyone to pursue a shared vision involves leading. The excitement generated by such a strategy can revitalize an organization and create leaders at every level.

Effective direction-setting requires strategic vision and the shaping of an institutional mission and philosophy compatible with the demands of the twenty-first century.

Strategic Vision. Strategic vision embraces the challenge of Herbert Troom's *Dissertation in Creativity:* "Nothing is done. Everything in the world remains to be done or done over. Nothing is known, positively and completely..." (*Administrator*, 1987). In an era of rapid change it is incumbent upon an organization to be adaptive and more future oriented—to face the future with all of its implications.

This will require executive leaders who are willing to unhook from the past, are able to draw new boundaries beyond the existing limits of ideas and activities, and are equal to the challenge of the information society—to foresee the alterations that technological breakthroughs may force on an organization. This has prompted Peters (1987) to call for a new theory of management, based upon the impact of changing technology on every aspect of the internal and external dealings of the organization.

Technology has greatly increased the amount of information available in the workplace without improving our ability to use it. When this happens, workers resist. And without worker support, "the value of newly introduced technology plummets" (Connor 1985).

"Unlike earlier waves of automation that merely allowed companies to process paperwork faster, the latest tools put vast arrays of facts and figures at a manager's fingertips. Literally thousands of documents can be culled electronically through outside databases, plus rigorous statistical analysis" (*Leadership Abstracts*, 1988). As the pace of technological change accelerates, chief executive officers must not only stay abreast of innovations, but also they must learn how to harness new technology to make better products and sharper decisions. The executive leader of tomorrow must be a master of technology.

The future will also require executive leaders to have a global perspective and to interpret the impact of international economic and demographic trends on the institution and its community. Executive leaders must be aware of emerging trends, issues, and new ideas; must know and use other "anticipatory" research techniques; and must be prepared by contingency planning for large-scale societal changes.

Philosophy and Mission. Successful institutions have philosophies that are simple and to the point, but that are lived with intensity. These philosophies are based on a deeply held personal vision of the future and a voluntary commitment to transform the institution's work environment. Fundamental to the clear and simple shared vision is a belief that each person can contribute to that vision.

According to Bennis (1985), successful executive leaders are visionaries who develop a clear sense of purpose or mission of the organization. In mission setting, the executive leader needs to unify diverse points of view and build consensus for the future direction. The biggest challenge facing executive leaders is not determining the vision of the future, but rather transmitting that vision into reality, philosophy into practice, mission into action, and purpose into goals, policies, and new methodologies. Conscientious efforts to get the message across at every level of the organization are critical to creating the trust and understanding so necessary in managing change.

According to Vaughan (1988), it is through the communication of the mission of the college to the institution's internal and external constituents that the "president instills a vision of what the institution is capable of becoming; it is through this function that the president in conjunction with the governing board defines the purpose of the institution."

Presidents interviewed earlier by Vaughan (1986), for example, identified establishing and interpreting the mission of the college as the most important of four leadership roles of the president. Vaughan noted, however, that presidents have often failed to interpret and articulate the community college mission effectively and consistently to its various constituents.

Organizational Environment

Kanter suggested in 1983 that if successful executive leaders have to be skilled at building coalitions, it is equally true that the "...environment in which they operate has to clear the way." The executive leader's new role, according to Naisbitt and Aburdene (1985) will be to cultivate and maintain an ideal organizational environment—one that fosters a spirit of cooperation, commitment, and personal initiative and motivation—one that is nourishing to personal growth and "entrepreneurship."

Several researchers have found that successful executive leaders were, in effect, students of their organizations who recognized that organizational environment both empowers and constrains its members. They were engaged by the task of analyzing and reconstructing the organization, changing its basic metabolism (Bennis and Nanus, 1985).

These successful executive leaders were willing to implement both the design of the organizational purpose and the required control systems through group alignment and realignment—each individual pursuing his or her own vision while simultaneously empowering the organization (Senge, 1987, p. 9). The alignment of the wants and needs, the aspirations and expectations of both the employee and the leader shifts the emphasis of leadership from control to commitment, allowing people to manage themselves (Burns, 1978). A group mind begins to operate in highly aligned groups, making it unnecessary to take a vote. The stability resulting from alignment is what John W. Gardner (Waterman, 1987) referred to as "stability in motion," constant interplay between stability and change.

Culture and Climate. If the 1970s was the decade of "strategic thinking," the 1980s will be remembered for the recognition of the immense impact of organizational culture and climate—the amalgam of shared values, mores, symbols, and ways of thinking and doing business—on the fortunes of the organization (Tunstall, 1987).

Organizational culture can be seen in the patterns of language, the distribution of power, and the myths and legends that give meaning to interpreted events (Birnbaum, 1988). Paramount to the success of both business and education organizations is the development of a distinct and pervasive culture. Such an organizational value system is based on concern for people—respect for human dignity that is caring and trusting.

If caring is demonstrated by the executive leader through nurturing gestures, it produces a communal process where the workplace is viewed as a community or a family. And "trust is not only the glue that holds the human group together, but when it dissolves, the capacity of the group to function effectively is seriously impaired" (Gardner, 1987, p. 15). Trust, then, is essential to teamwork. Conscientiously building trust with employees leads to a healthy state of employee morale.

Culture permeates everything in the organizational environment and exerts a powerful influence. Culture can facilitate or frustrate organizational change, support or jeopardize strategic planning, and unify or divide staff. It also affects how employees work. Ambiguous or inconsistent cultures yield indecisive behaviors, counterproductive activities, declining productivity, and employee frustration. Strong adaptive cultures can unify work efforts, increase productivity, and enhance satisfaction. Accordingly, in all successful organizations there is a continual effort to sustain and enhance the organizational culture.

Successful organizations are also characterized by a climate where people not only can develop the capacity to determine their own destiny, but also can have a direct influence on, and are directly rewarded from, the success of "their organization." Such organizations are headed by executive leaders who believe that work should be meaningful in a rich and positive sense and recognize that their interpersonal behavior is one of the most important factors in creating organizational climate. Such organizations are characterized by excellence, adaptability, and continuous learning; they encourage leadership at all levels of the organization; and they treat everyone as a source of creative input. They "reward failure" and use symbolic behavior in directing visual attention to successful members of the team. Successful executive leaders are more often heromakers than heroes. They recognize that the "joy of success" is sharing the credit for accomplishments. Peters and Waterman (1982) have provided numerous ways to turn the "supporting cast" into heroes through "celebration" and "famous bragging sessions."

Underscoring the importance of organizational climate, the Commission on the Future of Community Colleges suggested that community be defined ". . . not only as a region to be served, but also a climate to be created in the classroom, on the campus, and around the world" (American Association of Community and Junior Colleges, 1988, p. 7).

In 1976 Bennis described the future executive leader as the "social architect of the corporate culture, whose primary responsibility would be to guide the employees through the multiple-option decision making process of the information society" (p. 165). Several writers have determined that future "social architects" will need to communicate openly and live by a strong value system themselves, establishing an environment where individual and organizational value systems are compatible. Most individuals are value-driven, and they can be motivated to live up to organizational values if these are clearly communicated by both the practice and the preaching of the leader (Parnell, 1988).

As the social architect of the organizational culture, the future executive leaders will need to understand how society's stereotypical views affect careers and personal lives. Kanter's 1977 research determined that future leaders need to develop internal environments that support both majority and minority "corporate cultures."

According to Roueche, Baker, and Rose (1988), the "molding and shaping of a new community college culture is clearly and visibly the domain of the community college president" (p. 52).

108

Use of Power. While writers have debated whether leadership is characterized by the exercise of power or the ability to empower and motivate others to assume leadership, all agree that successful executive leaders understand the wise use of power. The empowering process—inspiring and motivating others to action—is an essential part of translating vision into reality, according to Srivastva (1986).

According to Kanter (1977), leadership is determined by the extent of power the leader possesses, both external and internal to the system; power is the ability to command a favorable share of resources, opportunities, and rewards for followers. The power broker, according to Kanter, has a greater command of organizational resources, a greater access to decision makers, a greater "credibility," and a greater effectiveness than others within the organization. Fisher (1984) concluded that "the leader who combines charismatic power with expert and legitimate power, adding a small measure of reward power with little or no coercive power, achieves maximum effectiveness" (p. 40).

Empowering others to higher performance levels and involving others in the decision making process is a mark of a successful leader, according to Governor Madeline Kunin of Vermont (Day, 1986). Accordingly, John Sculley, CEO of Apple Computers, has defined the role of the CEO as providing the framework and resources for bright people to do great things (Raymond, 1986). A common characteristic of successful executive leaders is their ability to empower and excite others; they invoke a magnetism that attracts and energizes others to them.

Organizational Design and Structure. One of the areas most affected by the accelerating rate of social change is organizational design and structure. The classical hierarchical organization may become only a historical artifact of our civilization. According to McCune (1986), ". . . information tools are changing the nature of work itself, the structure of organizations, the relationship of employees to organizations and their work, and the type of products and services produced" (p. 5). The computer has enormous potential for refining organizational structure; crucial operating data can be provided to front-line workers by "smart machines." "You've got to leave the hierarchy out of it," according to Harvard labor expert Shoshana Zuboff, "and give information to those who deal with customers so they can make flexible, rapid decisions" (*Leadership Abstracts*, 1988).

Accordingly, the flow of information in successful organizations regarding the changing context and environments within which the organization operates is from bottom to top. Only information pertinent to overall business is demanded by the top, and local decision making powers reside with the local managers themselves.

"To survive and prosper in the decade ahead, organizations must restructure outmoded systems and styles of management to fit the needs and abilities of a new work force and to meet increased world competition," according to speakers at a symposium titled, "The Organizations in the Decade Ahead" (Senge, 1987). Organizations must create personal opportunities, rewards, and challenges for their employees.

In response to this challenge and consistent with the major trend toward decentralization, successful organizations are deliberate bureaucracy-busters, removing many levels of the hierarchical pyramid and spreading far more authority across the organizational spectrum. They have flatter organizational structures and open communication systems and provide for the decentralization of power. The removal of layers of management eliminates staff and pushes decisions down, localizing "job ownership" and "entrepreneurship" to the fullest extent possible.

The top-down authoritarian management style, according to Naisbitt and Aburdene (1985), is yielding to a looser, more informal and professional style—a networking style of management, where power and opportunity are distributed widely, where people learn from one another horizontally, where everyone is a resource for everyone else, and where each person gets support and assistance from many different directions. Decentralization fosters a participative style of management where there is a clear link between efforts and rewards. Employees work with managers to solve organizational problems, are given a large degree of flexibility, and are encouraged to provide input so that managers can make more informed and intelligent decisions. "We just take the coach approach," explained Averitt CEO Gary Sasser. "Lots of feedback, lots of encouragement; our people do the rest" (*Leadership Abstracts*, 1988). Divisions in these lean and fluid organizations are kept small—to a few hundred people—and run as highly autonomous units (Waterman, 1987). People move more often and with greater degrees of freedom across function, division, from line to staff, and vice-versa. Promotion from within is the rule with additional key skills brought in when needed from the outside.

Successful organizations also have found ways to break up a larger organization into relatively small, free-standing units, even with their own internal boards of directors. They keep all members of the organization "close to the customer" and in touch with new technological developments.

The ideal is a network of small "organizations within the large organization." These free-standing units are highly autonomous, providing maximum independence for people who are essentially free to grow their own businesses. Local managers are empowered with authority to make a difference in the governance of these "entrepreneurial enclaves."

Successful organizations also rely heavily on the use of teams and task forces. Teamwork, however, is a tricky business; it requires people to pull together toward a set of shared goals or values, because teams today do not simply advise; they act (Waterman, 1987). Multi-dimensional problems require cross-functional solutions. A team can focus a vast array of expertise and experience on problem diagnosis and resolution; sound teamwork can compress time and enable a group to achieve results quickly.

Several recent books provide corporate models of innovative organizations of the future: *In Search of Excellence* by Thomas J. Peters and

Robert Waterman (1982); *The Change Masters: Innovation for Productivity in the American Corporation* by Rosabeth Moss-Kanter (1983); *Innovation and Entrepreneurship: Practice and Principles* by Peter F. Drucker
(1985); *A Passion for Excellence: Leadership Difference* by Thomas J.
Peters and Nancy Austin (1985); *The Renewal Factor* by Robert Waterman (1987); and *Thriving on Chaos* by Thomas Peters (1987).

Revitalization and Renewal

Mobilizing and focusing the energy necessary for institutional revitalization and individual renewal is one of the greatest challenges facing the
future executive leader (Tichy and Ulrich, 1985). This requires a philosophy of leadership that has been described as "servant leadership"—leading
people by serving them.

Greenleaf (1977), concerned with the failure of educational institutions to nurture leaders and understand the nature of followers, theorized
that the servant leader's primary concern is whether the followers grow
as persons; that is, whether while being served they become healthier,
wiser, more autonomous, and willing to serve others.

"Organizations exist for only one purpose: to help people reach ends
together that they could not achieve individually." It should not be beyond
the purview of organizational leadership to "grow" qualities that do not already exist (Waterman, 1987). Successful organizations strike a balance, using
training programs and mentors to polish young executives' rough edges.

Institutional revitalization requires environmental change and institutional response, during which the executive leader provides the steward-
ship necessary to help institutional members work through the psycho-
dynamics of change (Tichy and Ulrich, 1985). And individual renewal is
widely recognized as a focus of leadership. According to Waterman (1987),
the renewal factor needs to be built into every organization to keep the
competitive edge.

"The president's success, and thus the institution's success, rest with
his or her ability to maximize the potential of each person" in an environment of ambiguity and change (Roueche, Baker, and Rose, 1988, p. 51).
Being committed to the development of human potential, the president
is able to motivate and inspire faculty and staff and to provide them with
opportunities to be creative and on the "cutting edge," by stretching and
encouraging them to make meaningful contributions. Renewal is fostered
through training and mentoring, the sponsorship of others.

Institutional revitalization and renewal requires that executive leaders
be teachers, lifelong learners, and role models and mentors.

Teacher. The recent literature on change and renewal recognizes that
one of the major responsibilities of the leader is to be a teacher. Executive leaders perform as teacher, coach, counselor, and guide. They help
their subordinates learn specific tasks and develop management skills—
such as judgment, communication, and working independently.

Recognizing that the success of almost every organization today depends on its ability to meet the challenges and demands placed on it, the executive leader teaches the values, mission, goals, and objectives of the enterprise continuously.

Lifelong Learning. Future executive leaders must be willing to commit to the idea of lifelong learning for themselves and others. This role is consistent with the future trend toward a "blended life plan."

Those executive leaders studied by Bennis and Nanus in 1986 showed an "amazing appetite" for continuous self-learning and development. Describing the leaders as lifelong learners, these authors observed that they have the capacity to learn, be self-reflective (which enables them to play a self-renewal leadership role), and keep abreast of new developments and advancements. They use outside training, in-house training, and consultants to achieve this end.

If executive leaders are not open to learning, Alstadt (1985) reported, neither change nor innovation will occur; leaders who exhibit curiosity and a willingness to learn provide a role model and inspiration for their followers.

Role Model and Mentor. Most people desire to be associated with a "rising star." Even the most sophisticated people are influenced by association with such executive leaders, and will go to extreme lengths to gain their acceptance.

When executive leaders serve as role models and mentors, they symbolize the group's unity and identify. Duncan (1988) reported that mystery—"certain 'auras' or images—revolves around these leaders, causing writers to refer to them as legends, and causing followers to be attracted to them and to be willing to commit themselves to their direction;" she quoted Naisbitt and Aburdene (1985), Tichy and Davanna (1986), Raymond (1986), and Greenleaf (1987). Since the executive leader's behavior is imitated by others in the institution, the extent to which they carry out the mission of the institution is often linked to the leader's success as a mentor.

Peters and Austin suggested in 1985 that this mystery surrounding executive leaders emanates from the followers' impressions that the leader will be able to influence and reflect their hopes, dreams, and aspirations. The single greatest lever of cultural innovation is the desire of most employees to follow their leader's examples. Accordingly, Henry Mintzberg has called the CEO the role model of the organization (Bennis, 1976). The behavior of executive leaders as role models is even more important than the values and vision expressed through direction setting. The behavior of executive leaders sends out signals to their constituencies. Harold Lasswell has referred to the "flow of images" that surrounds individuals and institutions. Over time these images create impressions that, taken in the aggregate, become the basis for appraisals of judgments of the person or institution (Cunningham, 1985).

Executive leaders also play a mentoring role, recognizing it as an effective means to assure continuity and pass on to the next generation a particular brand of leadership. They understand what kind of person the subordinate wants to become and then support personal growth. The subordinate's progress reflects the manager's effectiveness. Mentoring is an active process involving guidance, direction, sharing, and nurturing by one who is more experienced. A mentoring relationship requires careful thought, planning, and, specifically, careful matching of mentors and mentees (Caine, 1988). Some individuals are mentored more by events, situations, or circumstances than by a particular relationship with one specific person (Darling, 1985).

Finally, Birnbaum (1988) has offered five simple ways for community college executive leaders to become more effective:

- *"Complicate yourself.* The world is complicated, and it is possible to interpret any situation from a number of perspectives any or all of which may provide useful administrative insights...complex administrators can draw on numerous explanations and frameworks to find actions to suit particular situations...only complicated minds can see the many and conflicting realms of complicated situations.

- *Know your followers.* Leaders are constrained by the limits imposed by their followers. Leaders who exceed these limits will suffer a reduction in their status and lose their claim to leadership...leaders must do what followers want, even when the followers do not know that they want it! To know what followers want, it is important to encourage open communication and then to listen.

- *Check your cognitive biases.* Leaders are likely to believe themselves to have more positive influence than they really do, to cognitively disassociate themselves from failures and, like everyone else, to make self confirming errors of judgment about cause and effect...to increase their effectiveness leaders should encourage dissent on their staff, should find value and conflict, and should accept criticism nondefensively.

- *Increase your power.* Power is the ability to influence others. Of the five types of social power, legitimate power is set by our organizational role, and referent power is related to our personality (both comparatively difficult to change). Reward power has variable effects, and coercive (punitive) power creates alienation. This leaves one power base to our manipulation—expert power. ...one school of thought says that leaders will be more effective as they develop a repertoire of management, personnel, educational, and public relations skills. Another says that effectiveness depends not upon the skills themselves but upon others' perceptions that one is skilled. But in either case, expertise gives followers a sense of confidence and increases their willingness to follow, and that may increase institutional prestige and support among important external constituencies.

- *Be equally concerned with substance and process.* In most colleges and universities the prevailing mood for most substantive matters is apathy—most people are not concerned about most issues most of the time. But one thing they are almost certain to be concerned about is process, because their right to participate and get involved is linked to their organizational status. . . in higher education, process is substance, and leaders who forget that are likely to generate opposition to even the best ideas" (pp. 149–151).

References

Administrator, "Education's Future Linked to Critical Agenda" 6(23) (December 14), 1987.

Alstadt, Donald M., "Institutionalizing Leadership: The Strategic Committee of the Board," *Selections From New Management.* University of Southern California Graduate School of Business, 1985.

American Association of Community and Junior Colleges, "Building Communities: A Vision for a New Century," A Report of the Commission on the Future of Community Colleges, (Washington, D.C.: AACJC), 1988.

Baldridge, J. Victor; Curtis, David V.; Ecker, G.; and Riley, G.L., *Policy Making and Effective Leadership: A National Study of Academic Management* (San Francisco, CA: Jossey-Bass), 1978.

Bennis, Warren, "A Personal Reflection: Peter Drucker" *New Management* 2(3) (Winter 1985): 21–26.

Bennis, Warren, *The Unconscious Conspiracy* (New York, NY: AMACOM), 1976.

Bennis, Warren, "The Wallenda Factor" *Selections from New Management,* University of Southern California Graduate School of Business, 1985.

Bennis, Warren and Nanus, Burt, *Leaders* (New York, NY: Harper and Row), 1985.

Birnbaum, Robert, "The Reality and Illusion of Community College Leadership," in Eaton, Judith S., (ed.) *Colleges of Choice: The Enabling Impact of the Community College* (New York, NY: ACE/Macmillan), 1988.

Caine, R., "Mentoring the Novice Clinical Nurse Specialist" *Clinical Nurse Specialist,* in press 1988.

Cleveland, Harland, *The Future Executive* (New York, NY: Random House), 1972.

Cohen, Michael D., and March, James G., *Leadership and Ambiguity: The American College President* (New York, NY: McGraw-Hill), 1974.

Connor, Daryl R., "Introducing New Technology Humanely" *Training and Development Journal* 39(5) (May 1985): 33–36.

Cunningham, Lavern L., "Leaders and Leadership: 1985 and Beyond" *Phi Delta Kappan* 67(1) (September 1985): 17–20.

Darling, L.W., "So You've Never Had a Mentor. . . Not to Worry" *The Journal of Nursing Administration* 14(5): 43–44.

Day, N., "Madeleine Kunin" *Working Woman* (July 1986): 74–77.

Desruisseaux, Paul, "Gardner on Leadership: Probing How to Deal with a World of 'Multiple, Colliding Systems' " *Chronicle of Higher Education* 33(7) (January 1987).

Duncan, Ann Huberty, "A Study to Identify Desired Leadership Competencies for Future Chief Executive Officers of American and Junior Colleges" doctoral dissertation, Pepperdine University, California, 1988.

Fisher, James, *Power of the Presidency* (New York, NY: Macmillan), 1984.

Fryer, Jr., Thomas W., "An Overarching Purpose for Institutional Governance" *Leadership Abstracts* 1(11) (July 1988): 1–2.

Greenleaf, Robert, *Servant Leadership* (Ramsey, NJ: Paulist Press), 1977.

Joseph, Earl, "Earl Joseph Predicts: Training is a Growth Industry" *Training* 21 (10) (October 1984): 133–135.

Kanter, Rosabeth Moss, *Men and Women of the Corporation* (New York, NY: Basic Books), 1977.

Kanter, Rosabeth Moss, *The Change Masters* (New York, NY: Simon and Schuster), 1983.

Leadership Abstracts, "The 21st Century Executive" abstracted from *U.S. News and World Report* 1(8) (April 1988): 1–2.

McCune, Shirley D., *Guide to Strategic Planning for Education* (Alexandria, VA: Association for Supervision and Curriculum Development), December 1986.

Martel, Leon, *Mastering Change* (New York, NY: Simon and Schuster), 1986.

Naisbitt, John and Aburdene, Patricia, *Reinventing the Corporation* (New York, NY: Warner Books), 1985.

Parnell, Dale, "Leadership is Not Tidy" *Leadership Abstracts* 1(4) (February 1988): 1–2

Peters, Tom, *Thriving on Chaos* (New York, NY: Alfred A. Knopf, Inc.), 1987.

Peters, Thomas J. and Austin, Nancy, *A Passion for Excellence: The Leadership Difference* (New York, NY: Random House), 1985.

Raymond, H. Allan, *Management in the Third Wave* (Glenview, IL: Scott, Foreman and Company), 1986.

Roueche, John E.; Baker III, George A.; and Rose, Robert R., "The Community College President as Transformational Leader: A National Study" *Community, Technical, and Junior College Journal* 58(5) (April/May 1988): 48–52.

Senge, Peter M., "New Management Enters the Mainstream" *Management World* 16(1) (January 1987).

Srivastva, Suresh, and Associates, *Executive Power* (San Francisco, CA: Jossey-Bass Publishers), 1986.

Tichy, Noel M. and Davanna, Mary Anne, "The Transformational Leader" *Training and Development Journal* 40(9) (August, 1986): 27–32.

Tichy, Noel M. and Ulrich, David, "The Challenge of Revitalization" *New Management* 2(3) (Winter 1985): 53–55.

Tunstall, W. Brooke, "Back to the Future" *New Management* 5(1) (Summer 1987): 4–9.

Vaughan, George B., "Bringing Focus to the Presidency" *Leadership Abstracts.* 1(6) (March, 1988): 1–2.

Vaughan, George B., *The Community College Presidency* (New York, NY: ACE/Macmillan), 1986.

Waterman, Jr., Robert, *The Renewal Factor: How the Best Get and Keep the Competitive Edge* (New York, NY: Bantam Books), 1987.

Whetten, David A., "Effective Administrators: Good Management on the College Campus" *Change* 38(43) (November/December, 1984): 38–43.

Whetten, David A., and Cameron, Kim S., "Administrative Effectiveness in Higher Education" *Review of Higher Education* 9(1) (January 1985): 39–45.

Ervin L. Harlacher is professor of higher education, Graduate School of Education and Psychology, Pepperdine University, Culver City, California.